THE
GOSPEL
in BONDS

THE
GOSPEL
IN BONDS

THE TRUE STORY OF A COURAGEOUS PREACHER
IMPRISONED IN THE SOVIET GULAGS FOR HIS FAITH

GEORGI VINS

LIGHTHOUSE TRAILS PUBLISHING
ROSEBURG, OREGON

Library of Congress Cataloging-in-Publication Data

Vins, G. P. (Georgi Petrovich), 1928-1998
  The gospel in bonds : the true story of a courageous preacher imprisoned in the Soviet gulags for his faith / Georgi Vins. -- First Lighthouse Trails Edition.
     pages cm
  Includes bibliographical references and index.
  ISBN 978-0-9895093-6-7 (softbound : alk. paper) 1. Vins, G. P. (Georgi Petrovich), 1928-1998 2. Baptists--Russia--Biography. I. Title.
  BX6495.V5.A3714 2014
  286'.1092--dc23
  [B]
                                        2014021718

Dedicated to Peter and Lydia Vins, who considered Jesus Christ the greatest treasure of their lives and proclaiming the Good News of salvation the highest calling of every Christian. Following this commitment led Peter to a martyr's death for Christ's sake—he was executed in a Soviet prison at the age of 39. Lydia's commitment to actively serve the Lord, suddenly a widow at age 30, never wavered; she passed on these eternal values to her son Georgi and later to her five grandchildren.

ALSO BY GEORGI P. VINS

Testament From Prison
(also titled Three Generations of Suffering)

Moscow Express: and Other Stories

Along the Path of Faithfulness

Konshaubi—Free on the Inside

From Poetry Notebook

Publisher's Note: The poems and sidebars in this book are written by Georgi Vins unless otherwise indicated.

CONTENTS

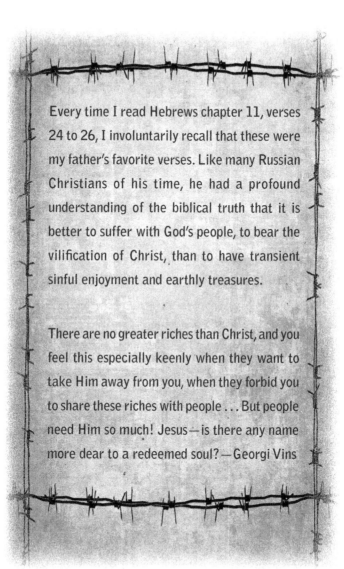

Every time I read Hebrews chapter 11, verses 24 to 26, I involuntarily recall that these were my father's favorite verses. Like many Russian Christians of his time, he had a profound understanding of the biblical truth that it is better to suffer with God's people, to bear the vilification of Christ, than to have transient sinful enjoyment and earthly treasures.

There are no greater riches than Christ, and you feel this especially keenly when they want to take Him away from you, when they forbid you to share these riches with people ... But people need Him so much! Jesus — is there any name more dear to a redeemed soul? — Georgi Vins

PROLOGUE

n 1926, an American missionary named Peter Vins left the United States for the mission field of Siberia. Young Peter had finished his seminary training in Kentucky, then for a time pastored a church of Russian immigrants in Pittsburgh, Pennsylvania. There he fell in love with a Christian woman and asked her to marry him. She agreed, and the two announced their engagement. However, when Peter told his fiancé that God was calling him to Russia, she refused to go along. Her ultimatum to him was "Either me, or Russia." So, broken-hearted, Peter called off the engagement and departed for Russia alone.

In Russia, the Lord's blessing was on Peter Vins. People responded to his preaching, and many joined the church. Also, before long, a Russian woman who was a dedicated Christian attracted his attention. Peter began courting young Lydia Zharikova and married her in 1927. In 1928, in the city of Blagoveschensk, Lydia bore her husband a son whom they named Georgi.

However, Peter Vins' hopes for a long life of ministry in Russia were not to be: the NKVD (secret police, forerunner of the KGB) began arresting Russian pastors and closing churches. They gave Peter Vins a choice—quit preaching and return to America or give up his American citizenship. He decided to stay and relinquished all rights as an American. In 1930, he was arrested and given a three-year term. When Peter was released, the authorities probably expected him to be too intimidated to continue teaching the Bible. But they were wrong. He continued meeting with small groups of believers, encouraging and edifying them despite the dark days of persecution. After a short time of freedom, he was re-arrested and held for nine months. A third arrest soon followed when dozens of fellow Christians were seized in the same night. This time he was sentenced to ten years of labor camp without the right of communication with his family. He never returned.

Years later, in answer to Lydia's repeated requests to authorities for knowledge about her husband, she received a statement that Peter had passed away in a labor camp on December 27, 1943. However, almost six decades later, in 1995, Georgi Vins was permitted to go to the KGB archives in Moscow and read the file the NKVD had kept on his father. Labeled "Top Secret," its pages revealed that the authorities executed his father with a bullet in August 1937 at the age of 39.

Georgi committed his life to the Lord and was baptized in Omsk Baptist Church in 1944. Two years later, Lydia moved with her son Georgi to Kiev, Ukraine where he graduated from the Kiev Polytechnical Institute as an electrical engineer.

In time, the Lord brought a young Christian woman named Nadia into Georgi's life. Their friendship grew into love, and the couple married on January 27, 1952. As the years passed, the Lord blessed them with five children of their own.

However, even though Soviet law required him to hold a secular job, in 1962 Georgi was ordained as a Baptist evangelist. Following in his father's footsteps, he began preaching at meetings of the persecuted church.

In the early 1960s, many laymen and pastors of "registered" Baptist churches (i.e., churches which the Soviet authorities allowed to function legally but only under supervision and within harsh guidelines that contradicted the Scriptures) determined to worship freely without the yoke of government interference in the life of the church. They began meeting independently in private homes, apartments, and even in the forests. Georgi Vins became one of the leaders of the movement, making him a special object of concern for the KGB. In 1966, he was arrested in Moscow and sentenced to three years imprisonment. He spent one year in Lefortovo Prison and two more performing hard labor in prison camps in the Ural Mountains.

After his release, Georgi Vins resumed his ministry. However, when he learned that the authorities were preparing a new case against him, he went underground, living clandestinely while traveling and ministering. In 1974, he was arrested again, this time sentenced to ten years. The story you are about to read is Georgi's account of his years spent in Soviet prisons.

PETER AND LYDIA VINS WITH THEIR SON GEORGI. ALTHOUGH THEY DIDN'T KNOW IT AT THE TIME, THIS WAS TO BE THEIR ONLY CHILD.

TO MY PERSECUTORS

My persecutors, I do not curse you,
And at this hour under the burden of the cross
I pray for you and bless you
With the simple humanity of Christ.

I am pure before you: by word and deeds
I have called you to good and to light.
I have so much wished that your hearts
Would be possessed by the lofty ideal of love.

But rejecting this kind summons
You answered with rabid enmity.
My persecutors, I do not curse you,
But I am saddened by your fate.

The immortal examples of history
Speak of the futility of persecution—
The fires of love and abundant faith
Burn enthusiastically through the whole land!

My persecutors, I do not curse you,
And at this hour under the burden of the cross
I pray for you and bless you
With the simple humanity of Christ.

—**Georgi P. Vins**
Anyusha Prison Camp
December 1968

I am continually with thee: thou hast holden me by my right hand. Thou shalt guide me with thy counsel, and afterward receive me to glory. Whom have I in heaven but thee? and there is none upon earth that I desire beside thee. My flesh and my heart faileth: but God is the strength of my heart, and my portion for ever. (Psalm 73: 23-26)

1

THE BIRDS

Few creatures can endure the harsh climate of Siberia's far north, where the winter temperature often drops as low as -74° F. By then, the birds have long since flown south to their winter feeding grounds in the Philippines and Japan. Only the hardy ravens and magpies remain behind. And the ever-present sparrows . . .

During the coldest times, the sparrow would cling to the sides of the barracks with their tiny claws, pressing their little bodies against the walls. There they stayed for hours. If I was very quiet, I could get close enough to see that their little eyes were closed as they rested. It was so pleasant for them. How fragile they seemed, how incongruous with the severity of our surroundings.

One day I took them some bread crumbs. Carefully I shook the crumbs out of my pockets onto the snowy ground. Before long, I was surrounded by a whole flock of sparrows and the crumbs disappeared in moments. The little birds eyed me expectantly, waiting for more. I showed them my empty hands: "I have nothing else. Tomorrow I'll try to bring you more."

After a while, the sparrows recognized me. Every time I went outside, they'd leave their precarious shelters and gather around me, waiting for their bread. There were more than I could count.

Gazing at the tiny birds, joy filled my heart as I remembered the words of the Lord Jesus Christ: "Are not two sparrows sold for a farthing? And one of them shall not fall on the ground without your Father. But the very hairs of your head are all numbered.

**Fear ye not therefore, ye are of more value
than many sparrows." (Matthew 10:29-31)**

Dear little birds, if you haven't been forgotten by God, then neither have I! And so it was during my years in bonds that I saw most clearly God's protection and His faithfulness to me and to His Word. What a privilege it is to belong to Him!

2

THE MOST DANGEROUS OF ALL

nvar and I were the only prisoners in the "raven," a black police van used to transport prisoners. He sat alone in a compartment meant to hold fifteen prisoners while I was handcuffed and locked behind the metal door of a tiny cell reserved for the most dangerous criminals. Two soldiers armed with machine guns guarded us. A heavy metal grille separated them from us.

The harsh Siberian climate had left its mark on the narrow asphalt road. The lurching, swaying raven slowed to a crawl as the driver tried to maneuver around massive potholes. Though it was mid-May, snow still covered much of the ground in this vast territory known as Yakutia, thousands of miles northeast of Moscow. Our destination: Bolshaya Markha, a strict regime labor camp in a remote region in the far north of Siberia.

Anvar shook his head in amazement. "Georgi, why do they treat you like this?" he shouted over the thunderous roar of the engine. A heavy accent thickened his Russian.

I'd met Anvar two weeks earlier in the prison at Irkutsk where we shared a cell. Then we spent ten days at a camp near the city of Yakutsk. Anvar was a stocky man of medium height. The gray stubble on his huge, shaved head seemed premature for a man in his mid-forties. A sharp eagle-like nose protruded over a coal-black mustache. Muslim by background, Anvar was fascinated that I was imprisoned for preaching the Gospel. We had spent many hours discussing the Bible and Jesus Christ.

Anvar openly admitted that he had killed the district attorney in the city of Baku, for which he was sentenced to fifteen years. He quickly earned a reputation among camp authorities for being a dangerous criminal. He had already stabbed one prisoner with a knife and struck another on the head with an iron bar. Anvar was usually handcuffed during transport and was surprised at being denied that "privilege." He turned to me again.

"Ha! It looks as though you are even more dangerous than I!" He shouted something else, but the words were lost under the engine's clamor. The isolation of my tiny cage made it useless for me to reply. Through the window in the door of my cell, I could see Anvar talking with the two soldiers. He kept pointing in my direction. The soldiers were very young. I knew they made no decisions about where or how to move me. Those orders came from the KGB. And to the KGB, I really was more dangerous than Anvar.

One prison camp director had told me, "You'd be better off if you were a thief or a murderer rather than a Christian!"

What will the next camp be like?, I wondered as I thought about the past week.

I had just spent ten days at camp Mokhsogollokh, near Yakutsk. Although the camp was as secure as a fortress, guards often fired random warning shots at night to discourage dreams of escape.

About a mile from the camp was a factory, which manufactured panels, flooring, and other components for the pre-fabricated buildings of the North. Like the camp, the factory was surrounded by massive wood fences topped with rolls of barbed wire. Armed

ONE OF THE SOVIET PRISON CAMPS IN WHICH GEORGI VINS WAS IMPRISONED

soldiers from the Ministry of the Interior, MVD, patrolled the area with specially trained German shepherd guard dogs.

About 2000 prisoners and 500 civilians worked in two shifts at the factory, which operated day and night. Each prisoner worked at least a ten-hour shift. Twice a day, morning and evening, the soldiers led out columns of 1000 prisoners, marching slowly the mile from the living zone of the camp to the factory.

When I got my assignment at the factory, the supervisor was glad to see me. He was a civilian, about twenty-five years old, with no technical training to qualify him as supervisor of the electrical division. He already knew I was an electrical engineer. "You can help us draw up blueprints for the factory and develop technical documentation. How we worked without blueprints and instructions—I have no idea!"

Prisoners have no choice about where they work or what they do. During my first sentence in the northern Ural Mountains (1966-1969), I had worked in the forest in a lumber camp. In the snowy winters, the temperature often dropped to -79 degrees F. The column of prisoners sank into the snow as we stomped a path to our work place. In the summer, the forest was a kingdom of mosquitoes and midges. There was no way to protect ourselves from the hordes of insects—not in the forest, not in the barracks. Our faces, necks, and arms were swollen from their merciless bites. In the spring and fall, our clothes and boots were always soaked, and our bodies were covered with painful boils from general weakness and colds brought on by the

GEORGI—1963, SHORTLY AFTER BEING RELEASED FROM HIS FIRST ARREST AT 34 YEARS OLD

miserable conditions and frequent downpours. Day after day we worked under the open sky, guarded by armed soldiers.

But Mokhsogollokh was much different. I was assigned to a bright, spacious room with a desk, drawing table, and a cabinet. How I rejoiced to have a few hours alone in this room! In the barracks the shouts, curses, quarrels, and fights of the other prisoners were a constant distraction, but at work I could set aside my blueprints for a while and pray in solitude.

I was also able to move freely about the plant to become familiar with the electrical equipment and the workers. Besides asking technical questions, I looked for other believers. Each time a man asked why I'd been arrested, I had another opportunity to share my faith in Jesus Christ.

A few days after I arrived at Mokhsogollokh, a KGB official summoned me to his office. He was thin, almost fragile in appearance, with a squeaky voice. His narrow eyes glittered with hostility.

"We know," he said testily, "that you want to build a secret printing press here at the camp to print religious brochures! We will not allow this! We'll rot you! We'll put you in the punishment block. You'll get solitary confinement!"

> "We know you're dangerous. Hundreds of eyes will scrutinize your every move. Don't you dare pray or talk to anyone about God!"

I was surprised. "I don't understand. What kind of print shop? What brochures?"

"Cut the act!" the officer barked, slamming the desk with his bony fist. "We know you're dangerous. Hundreds of eyes will scrutinize your every move no matter where you are in the camp, the barracks, or the factory. Don't you dare pray or talk to anyone about God!"

He struggled to sound ominous and produce a deep bass voice. The result was comical.

"It never occurred to me to set up a print shop here," I answered quietly. "Besides, it's impossible. But I do have the right to pray. I am a believer and will continue praying to God. I'll pray for the whole camp, and I'll pray for you, that the Lord would grant you repentance and the salvation of your soul."

"Don't you ever pray for my soul!" the officer shrieked. "You'll regret this conversation! Now get out of here!"

That's how I found myself in handcuffs and on my way to another camp. But I knew that my banishment from Mokhsogollokh was actually a victory for Christ. The KGB fears open prayers and open testimony about Jesus Christ more than the vilest crimes! As we rumbled along in the raven, I knew my future was secure in the Lord's trustworthy hands.

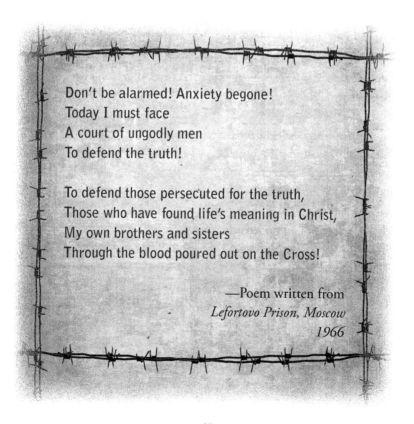

Don't be alarmed! Anxiety begone!
Today I must face
A court of ungodly men
To defend the truth!

To defend those persecuted for the truth,
Those who have found life's meaning in Christ,
My own brothers and sisters
Through the blood poured out on the Cross!

—Poem written from
Lefortovo Prison, Moscow
1966

3

GETTING PAST THE CONTROL POINT

At about ten o'clock that night, the raven finally ground to a halt. Our sixty-two-mile journey had taken nearly four hours. The soldiers let Anvar and me out of the van and took us to the control point. The handcuffs made it difficult for me to hold on to my small bag of personal belongings. Anvar looked at me and shook his head.

"Georgi," he whispered, "I'm a murderer, a criminal, and I don't have handcuffs. But you're an engineer and a believer and you have handcuffs? You didn't kill or knife anyone. You're a man of God. What they're doing is not good."

An officer and the camp director were working the control point. The convoy officer handed over our files. The director scanned the papers.

"Take them back!" he announced. "I won't accept them. I have enough cutthroats!"

"But I have orders to bring them here to Bolshaya Markha," protested the convoy officer.

"I won't take them," interrupted the director. "I know this man." He pointed to Anvar. "He's already been in every camp in the North!" Then he pointed to me. "And who's this? Why is he wearing handcuffs?"

"My orders say he travels only in handcuffs," answered the convoy officer.

The director looked at me. "Why were you arrested? What's your crime?"

"I'm a Christian," I replied. "I was sentenced to ten years for my faith in God."

"A Baptist?"

"Yes."

"Quite a pair we've got here," he muttered. "A murderer and a Baptist!" He turned to the convoy officer. "I won't accept them. The last thing I need is a Baptist agitator! Take them back."

The camp director turned and abruptly left the control point. The telephone was kept busy as both the duty officer and the convoy officer tried to resolve their dilemma. Anvar and I could do nothing but stand and wait. We were exhausted. We didn't care what camp we went to as long as it was soon so we could lie down and sleep.

Anvar approached the duty officer. "Citizen officer, let us sit down. We are very tired."

"Keep standing!" he barked. "Bandits like you and this Baptist should be shot, not chauffeured around from camp to camp!"

My handcuffs were starting to hurt and the slightest movement in my wrist automatically caused them to tighten. I decided to speak to the convoy officer.

"Citizen officer, please take off these handcuffs. They're very tight."

"Why not just pray to your God?" he taunted. "Maybe He'll take them off for you!"

I kept silent, trying not to move my hands. About an hour later, the camp director finally agreed to accept Anvar and me. My handcuffs were removed, and we were strip-searched. A guard took us to the barracks.

Bolshaya Markha, named after the nearby river, was considered a small labor camp with only 700 prisoners. Even so, the barracks

were crowded with up to 150 men each. The heavy, humid air made it difficult to sleep. Our metal bunk beds were covered with a thin cotton mattress and a tattered blanket. That's all we had, even on the coldest winter nights when the mercury plunged as low as -75°F. The food was bad, our bread tough and half-baked. But worst of all was the terrible water, heavy in salts and minerals and harmful to the health.

The prisoners worked in a brick factory right next to the living zone. The factory was situated on a low, swampy area surrounded by mud and water which kept our felt boots wet and our legs raw. The combination of harsh weather and poor conditions left us all sick most of the time.

During my first days at Bolshaya Markha, I had no way of writing to my family to let them know my new location. I had neither paper nor envelopes. I didn't even have a pen or pencil. I was surrounded by strangers.

One evening after work, I went into my barracks. It was the free hour just before lights out and most prisoners were smoking in the hallway or talking outside. Only two or three men were there. The man closest to me was lying on an upper bunk reading a tiny book. I recognized him from my work brigade.

I moved toward him to borrow a pen and paper.

He didn't notice me until I stood by his side, and in a flash his little book disappeared under his pillow. I had already seen the title. It was a Gospel!

My heart cried out, *Oh, great Lord, how amazing are Your ways! Your Word has reached even the darkest places on earth!*

But who was this young man? Was he a brother in Christ? Was he to be my friend? He, of course, knew nothing about me. To him I was just another new prisoner, and he was upset that I'd interrupted his secret occupation. Many questions were written on his face: What do you want from me? Who are you? Did you see my book? Are you going to report me?

"Excuse me," I said, not letting on that I'd noticed the book. "I came in on the last transport two days ago. I want to write to my family but don't have any paper, an envelope, or even a pen. Can you help me?"

"Sure," he answered, dropping lightly to the floor.

He was tall and skinny, about twenty years old, with an expressive face and alert brown eyes. His black prison pants and navy blue undershirt were clean and neat. Like all the prisoners, his head was shaved. From a small cabinet, he pulled a few sheets of paper, an envelope with a stamp, and a pen. As I thanked him, his suspicion began to melt.

"Where are you from?" he asked. "What are you in for?"

"I'm from Kiev," I replied, "and I'm a believer, a Baptist. I was sentenced to ten years for my faith. This is my second term. The first time I got three years in a camp in the northern Urals."

"For your faith?" he asked.

"Yes. And what are you in prison for? Also for faith?"

He hesitated. "No," he said cautiously. "For something else."

Just then a noisy group of prisoners entered the room. I nodded to my new acquaintance and went to write a letter.

How precious it is for any believer—especially one in a remote Siberian labor camp—to meet someone searching in God's Word for truth! This young man had not been imprisoned for his faith. Yet here he was, secretly reading a Gospel! How did he get it? What was going on in his heart? I knew I must pray for him.

GEORGI VINS
IN 1964 AS A
YOUNG PASTOR —
TWO YEARS
BEFORE HIS FIRST
IMPRISONMENT

4

VICTOR'S GOSPEL

The next evening I was able to talk again with my new acquaintance. His name was Victor. He was twenty-three and had been sentenced to fifteen years for robbing a bank. He still had twelve years to serve. Victor did not mention the Gospel, and our first conversation was brief, but he spoke warmly of his aunt, who was a believer.

Victor wrote to his aunt about me. She answered right away and in careful wording expressed her joy that a Christian was at the camp. She encouraged Victor to get to know me better. She was very concerned about Victor and wanted him to abandon his wild lifestyle and turn to Jesus Christ.

"Just think!" Victor exclaimed. "My aunt finished her studies at the university, then she became a Christian. When the authorities told her to choose between a career in teaching and God, she said 'God!' She was dismissed from her job and was never allowed to work in a school again."

I was interested. "When did that happen?"

"About twenty years ago," he answered. "Her husband was also a Christian. He was arrested just before the war and died in prison. I never saw him, but my mother and my aunt told me all about him. He was a Gospel preacher. My aunt says he was very good. Christians still talk about him."

"Did they have any children?" I asked.

"No. My aunt wanted to raise me after my father left us, but I didn't want to go live with her." Victor paused, a faraway look in his dark eyes. "I'm sorry now that I didn't. I'd be a different man today. I wouldn't be a criminal." He looked at me intently. "I really respect genuine believers."

"Victor, you can become a new man now—a believer in Christ! The Lord loves you. He died for you. He'll forgive your sins and give you a new life. Just put your faith in Him."

The next day Victor came to me. "I have a Gospel," he whispered. "Do you want to read it?"

"Thank you, Victor," I answered, "but I can't now. At least ten prisoners are watching every move I make and reporting to the KGB. Let's wait a while. Guard the Gospel for yourself."

But Victor said he had already shared it with another prisoner in his work brigade.

"How did you get it?" I asked.

Victor grinned slyly. "My aunt gave it to me during one of her visits last year. The guards didn't find it when they searched me after she left."

That night I thanked God for Victor's aunt and uncle. Through decades of hardship, people like them had carried the bright torch of the Gospel and remained faithful to Jesus Christ. How many such faithful heroes filled our churches! I thanked God for the Gospel now hidden in the camp. And I prayed that Victor would soon find a new life in Jesus Christ.

Two weeks after I arrived at Bolshaya Markha, there was a general all-camp search, the type usually conducted only once a year. Early Sunday morning all prisoners were ordered to take our personal belongings to the square in the center of the camp. Most of us had only a uniform, a warm jacket, an aluminum bowl and spoon, and a thin mattress and blanket.

We laid our meager possessions on the ground in front of the soldiers. As we stood at attention, the 21 soldiers sifted through the piles and frisked each prisoner, sometimes making one remove his shoes and outer clothing. Some were strip-searched by the officers or KGB workers. Meanwhile, other guards and soldiers searched through the barracks. Books, rags, papers, everything was thrown out onto a dump truck to be hauled away.

I was one of those searched by KGB officers. They went through all of my papers, my bedding, and footwear. Each seam of clothing was carefully felt as though they were looking for something specific.

Just as my search was completed, an officer in the opposite corner cried out, "A Gospel! A Gospel!" triumphantly waving the tiny book above his head. It was Victor's.

A camp official ran to Victor. "This is forbidden! Where did you get it? Who gave it to you?"

Victor just stood with his hands hanging limp at his sides. His face was pale. The other officers gathered excitedly around the Gospel.

One of them pointed at me. "That Baptist just got here and already he's spreading religious propaganda!"

Another officer approached me holding the Gospel. "Is this yours?"

"No."

"So how did it get here? Who brought it in?"

I kept silent.

"Why don't you speak?" he asked irritably.

"What crime is it to have a Gospel?" I asked. "It's God's Word. It's a book of grace and offers salvation to all people."

The officers again examined the Gospel, reading verses aloud. Just then the camp's highest-ranking KGB officer came.

"What's going on?" he asked. Someone handed him the Gospel. Slowly he turned the pages. He looked first at Victor, then at me, then back at Victor.

"So, whose Gospel is this, and how did it get into camp?"

No one spoke or even moved as the prisoners stood at attention. It was a beautiful, sunny day. The short Siberian summer had just begun. Brightly colored birds had just migrated north from the Philippines, Japan, and China. They were so free. Joyfully chirping, they rose to the sky, breaking the silence over our camp.

"It's mine," Victor said at last. "My aunt gave it to me when she came to visit last year."

The officers didn't believe him. But the search was now over and the prisoners returned to their barracks. A group of officers stayed behind, huddled around the little Gospel, reading verses aloud.

"Don't worry," Victor whispered as we walked back to our barracks. "I'll get another Gospel. I'll even get one for you!"

I pointed to the officers still looking at the little book. "They need to know about Christ, too. It's probably the first time in their lives they've ever held a Gospel."

Word about the Gospel quickly spread through the camp. Everyone thought it was mine. Many prisoners asked me what was written in it. Most of them had never even seen a Bible. One told me he'd collected Russian Bibles at international ports when he was a sailor. Others had heard Christian radio broadcasts from the West. The incident stirred up a lively interest in what God's Word had to say about China—would China take over the world? All this was at a time when tensions characterized the relationship between China and the Soviet Union. The most frequent questions I was asked were "Who is Jesus Christ? What does the Gospel say about life after death?" Before long, a small group of prisoners wanted me to teach them more about the Gospel.

"Oh, if we only had a Gospel of our own!" they mourned. "What you're saying is really interesting, but it would be so much better if we could read it ourselves!"

I prayed that God would prepare a way to bring His Word into our camp. I had no idea that greater difficulties lay ahead for me, especially after they found Victor's Gospel.

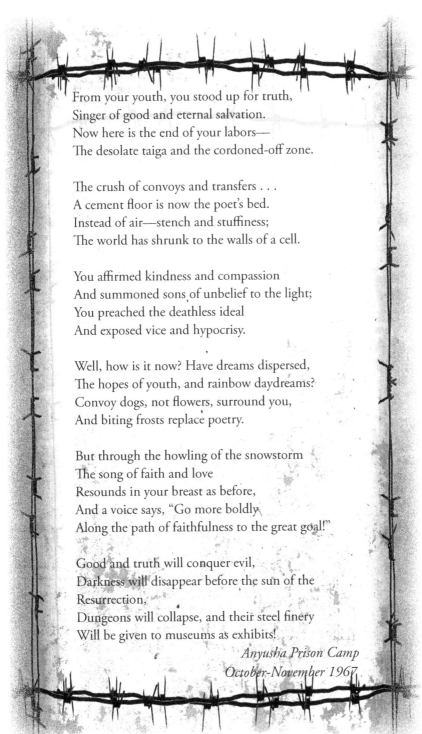

From your youth, you stood up for truth,
Singer of good and eternal salvation.
Now here is the end of your labors—
The desolate taiga and the cordoned-off zone.

The crush of convoys and transfers . . .
A cement floor is now the poet's bed.
Instead of air—stench and stuffiness;
The world has shrunk to the walls of a cell.

You affirmed kindness and compassion
And summoned sons of unbelief to the light;
You preached the deathless ideal
And exposed vice and hypocrisy.

Well, how is it now? Have dreams dispersed,
The hopes of youth, and rainbow daydreams?
Convoy dogs, not flowers, surround you,
And biting frosts replace poetry.

But through the howling of the snowstorm
The song of faith and love
Resounds in your breast as before,
And a voice says, "Go more boldly
Along the path of faithfulness to the great goal!"

Good and truth will conquer evil,
Darkness will disappear before the sun of the
Resurrection,
Dungeons will collapse, and their steel finery
Will be given to museums as exhibits!

Anyusha Prison Camp
October-November 1967

5

THE RED STRIPE

To make my conditions at camp even harder and to monitor every minute of my time, the KGB officials and the camp director declared me a dangerous prisoner likely to try to escape from camp. That proclamation earned me "the red stripe," a wide red ink mark stamped diagonally across my documents.

I was informed of this change in my status when I was called to the control point over the camp loudspeaker one evening after work. The duty officer and several others were waiting for me.

"According to an administrative decision and the Office of Corrective Labor Reform," the duty officer announced solemnly, "you have been designated by a red stripe as a person prone to escape. Effective immediately, we will be controlling and monitoring your every move."

He explained the new requirements. I had to report to the control point every two hours except during lights out. I was assigned a new cot in a special section near the barracks entrance together with other "escapees"—those who had either already tried to escape or were caught preparing to do so. Periodically throughout the night,

GEORGI VINS

guards would check my bed. I was to sleep only on my back with my face exposed.

"Do you understand these requirements?" the officer asked.

I was speechless.

"Well, you've played around with your faith, and now you have the red stripe. Now everyone will know that you're a dangerous criminal!" ridiculed another officer.

"But I'm not planning to escape! I'm not a criminal. I'm a Christian," I protested. "How am I dangerous in this camp? I've never heard of a Christian getting a red stripe. I would like to see the orders and read them for myself."

The officer laughed hoarsely. "Who would give the operative instructions to a prisoner? What a naive request!"

But I stood my ground. "Citizen officer, did you read those orders yourself?"

He shifted uncomfortably. "My orders are to tell you about the red stripe."

I turned to the others. "Citizen officers, did any of you read the orders?"

Everyone was silent. Then one of them shouted, "Vins, what are you doing? Are you refusing to obey? You are a criminal in the eyes of the law! You have a red stripe. You're going to try to escape. Be very careful, because if you make the slightest move in that direction, the soldiers will shoot without warning! Only ten men in this camp have the red stripe, and you're one of them."

"As a Christian, I'm obliged to obey the authorities in everything except my faith. So I will meet all of your requirements regarding the red stripe," I answered. "But I assure you that I am not planning to escape. This decision about the red stripe is not yours. It's not even the camp administration's decision. This was decided by the KGB in Moscow, and I consider this evidence that an attempt will be made on my life!"

The officers, who had been seated, suddenly leaped to their feet. They all spoke at once, interrupting each other. "What's he talking

36

about? Who's ever heard of such a thing? Why does he say that Moscow and the KGB are trying to kill him?"

I remained at attention, as prisoners must. The officers surrounded me, furiously defending the KGB. "What does the KGB or Moscow have to do with this? We're the ones who decided to give you the red stripe! Your faith is more dangerous than any crime!"

Then the senior officer turned to me. "Enough!" he bellowed. "Get back to the barracks! Move your things to your new cot. You'll be told where it is. At 9:55 tonight, five minutes before lights out, come here and report to me. You'll report here every night before bed."

When I got back to the barracks, I found that my things had already been moved to a cot near the door. That night, just before lights out, I walked across the camp grounds to the control point.

"Citizen officer, prisoner Vins checking in."

The officer pulled out a log book where my name was already recorded. He duly noted that I was at the camp and had not yet escaped. Then I returned to the barracks. Before going to sleep, I prayed and committed my life again to the Lord. Soon the lights were out and the fifty men in my section of the barracks were asleep. I lay on my back as I'd been ordered. Although I usually slept on my side, I could do nothing except try to get used to the new demands.

I don't know how long I'd been sleeping when a bright light shining in my face woke me up.

"What's your name?" A soldier was shaking my shoulder. I had forgotten about my red stripe and the required checks.

"My name?" I repeated sleepily.

Last name, first name, patronymic, date of birth. The soldier checked the documents in his hand.

"Why are you on your side? Sleep on your back!" he ordered as he moved away.

I fell asleep immediately, but soon someone was again shaking me by the shoulder.

"Up!" the soldier commanded. "Why are you sleeping on your side? Only on your back! Your face has to be visible!"

Last name, first name, patronymic, date of birth—and so it went several times throughout the night.

Everyone was up at six o'clock the next morning. I was exhausted. I had to go back to the control point again to notify the duty officer that I had not escaped.

Night after night, I was awakened by the light in my face and warnings not to sleep on my side. If only I could sleep through the night! Each day a ten-hour shift at the brick factory awaited me along with checking in every two hours at the control point.

It wasn't long before Christians heard about my desperate situation and sent out a prayer alert across our country and even abroad. This led to a curious misunderstanding in the West. A Christian mission in California heard about the red stripe and reported that the camp director had put a red stripe on my forehead and across my face with indelible ink! Actually, the stripe appeared only on my official documents and the identification card hanging over my cot. Even so, that red stripe gave me no peace, day or night.

How to die . . . one must also know this . . .
Not as a crushed, pitiful worm,
Not as a slave, not daring to dare—
But as a fighter against unbelief!

So that as I go along the narrow road
I will give myself to Christ with my whole soul,
And never fraternize in the slightest
With injustice, perfidy, and evil.

Hoisting the sail of radiant faith,
I shall race to my longed-for homeland,
And look into the eyes of Christ,
Who has stretched out His hand to life!

I shall say with a smile to my dear ones:
"My darlings . . . but tears are not needed!
I shall wait in Heaven for you,
The conquerors of death and hell."

In the vivid light of eternal day
Jesus Himself will embrace me,
And no one, my friends, will ever
Take away from me eternal life!

—Anyusha Prison Camp
January 1968

Thy word is true from the beginning: and every one of thy righteous judgments endureth for ever. Princes have persecuted me without a cause: but my heart standeth in awe of thy word. (Psalm 119: 160-161)

6

"DON'T TOUCH THAT DIAL!"

"Up! Up! All prisoners prepare for transport immediately!" the voice crackled over the loudspeaker. It was four o'clock in the morning. The sleepy camp suddenly bustled with activity as soldiers and officers ran into the barracks, rushing the prisoners. "Get out! Look alive!"

"Now what? Where are they taking us?" the prisoners asked each other. "Why the whole camp?"

If anyone knew, they didn't say.

One prisoner joked, "Probably Moscow has ordered us all to be shot! They're tired of dealing with criminals!" He spoke in a loud whisper after making sure no officers were nearby.

Another prisoner picked up on the theme. "We're done for, guys. China has attacked us. Now everybody in the camp is going to be shot!"

When all the prisoners had cleared the barracks, large trucks rumbled into the camp. As their names were called out, the prisoners climbed onto the trucks, which roared off into the darkness. Those of us with the red stripe were separated from the rest and put into a special van to be taken away under guard.

We reached our destination in less than an hour. The entire camp had been moved to Tabaga, just fifteen miles from the city of Yakutsk. Tabaga, named after the nearby river that flowed into the Lena, was the site of a large sawmill where 1200 to 1500 prisoners worked. I was assigned to work as an electrician. The equipment was in terrible condition, and the entire mill was often shut down because of electrical problems.

My red stripe followed me to Tabaga, and every two hours I had to report to the control point. It was normally a twenty-minute walk from my work area, but I had to run to make it in time. Life was very hard.

Tabaga's head KGB officer summoned me regularly for questioning. He tried to convince me to renounce God.

"God is just the invention of ignorant people," he'd say scornfully. "Who believes in God nowadays? There is no God! Why are you trying to revive religion? There's no room for religion in our society. Your faith belongs to yesterday. It's stupid to waste your life on some non-existent God. You're an engineer. You graduated from a Soviet institute. You've studied Marxism-Leninism. Why have you dedicated your life to propagandizing religion? Look where that got you. You're a prisoner—not just an ordinary prisoner but one disgraced with a red stripe. At the rate you're going, you'll never be free again! Make your choice—either God or freedom!" And on it went.

He had many such discussions with me in the evenings after work. I realized it was useless to try to explain things to him. Every time I started to say something, he would interrupt, ridiculing what I hold sacred. "I don't believe you, and I don't believe in your God.

42

There's no way out of this camp for you!" he repeated.

Those were very hard times, and my heart cried out to God. Bible verses kept coming to memory. "How amiable are thy tabernacles, 0 Lord of Hosts! My soul longeth, yea, even fainteth for the courts of the Lord: my heart and my flesh crieth out for the living God" (Psalm 84:1-2). "Thou tellest my wanderings: put thou my tears into thy bottle: are they not in thy book?" (Psalm 56:8). "I know that thou canst do every thing, and that no thought can be withholden from thee" (Job 42:2). I was hungry for His Word and fellowship with His people. It was during this stressful time that the Lord comforted me in an unusual way.

One cold winter night the head prisoner in our barracks woke me from a deep sleep. "Hurry!" he whispered urgently. "Get up! The duty officer is calling you to the control point."

"What happened?" I asked, suddenly alert.

"I don't know. He ordered you to go immediately!"

I dressed quickly. I noticed that it was one o'clock in the morning. Outside a sharp wind drove icy needles of snow into my face and hands. How lonely everything looked! Never had I felt so forlorn, so abandoned in that strange prisoner world. It was as though nothing existed except the desolate camp, nothing but prisoners and guards, pressure and slavery. Questions chased each other through my mind. *Why was I called in the middle of the night? What's the rush? Am I being moved to another camp? What awaits me?* My tired legs longed to carry me back to the barracks and the relative warmth of my cot.

The duty officer and several soldiers were waiting at the control point. I tried to read their faces to see what was happening, but they told me nothing. "Follow me." The tall, heavyset duty officer nodded toward his office.

He opened the door. On his desk sat a shortwave radio. I was amazed to hear the melody of "What a Friend We Have in Jesus," one of my favorite songs, playing softly.

The officer kept the volume low. "Sit down," he invited.

I sat close to the radio.

"This is a two-hour broadcast. Do you want to stay and listen?"

GEORGI VINS IN 1963 WITH HIS WIFE AND THREE CHILDREN (PETER AND NATASHA—BACK; LISA—FRONT) AFTER HIS BEING RELEASED FROM HIS FIRST ARREST, BEING JAILED FOR FIFTEEN DAYS. IT WAS CUSTOMARY FOR PRISONERS TO HAVE THEIR HEADS SHAVED

"Oh, of course! Thank you!" I was confused but elated. My weariness had disappeared.

"Just don't touch the radio," the officer warned, "and don't move the dial to Voice of America."

After he left, I knelt and prayed. That Christian program was exactly what I needed. I thanked the Lord for this special gift. Sermons, Christian songs, hymns, and prayers filled the room. When one half-hour program ended, another began. When a preacher prayed, I stood and prayed with him. When the choir sang, I sang along softly. My soul was so hungry for those sermons full of the testimony of Christ, of His love, His wisdom. Our Lord is truly wonderful! At the most difficult time in my camp life, He got me into that office to hear Christian radio programs.

From time to time the door opened and the duty officer looked in. "How's the reception?" he'd ask.

"Fine, thank you," I'd answer with a smile.

I enjoyed two hours there before the broadcast ended. Five minutes later the officer came in and turned off the radio.

"Well, what do you think? Did you like what you heard?" he asked, taking a seat across from me.

"Oh, I enjoyed it very much. Thank you. What excellent programs! What a treat!"

His eyes studied me intently. "How long have you been a Christian?"

"Since I was sixteen," I answered. "I'm forty-seven now. I've been following Jesus Christ for more than thirty years."

"Were your parents Christians, too?"

"Yes. My father was a Gospel preacher in America and then in Siberia. When I was just two years old, he was arrested for preaching and was sentenced to three years imprisonment. In 1937, he was arrested again. My father died in a concentration camp. Not long ago my mother, at the age of sixty-four, was also arrested and imprisoned for her faith." And I told the officer the story.

"How is your mother now? Is she home?"

"Yes. I hope to see her if she can make the long trip here to visit me."

The officer shook his head. "You have a very strange faith! Prison after prison!" he said softly, speaking half to himself. Then he led me out of his office and sent me back to the barracks.

Christian songs rang in my heart as I walked across the deserted camp zone. Snow was still falling, and the north wind was still blowing. But instead of burning my face, the snowflakes swirled lightly on their journey to the ground. They seemed to float in rhythm to the harmony of a great heavenly choir! I had just been at a worship service, where the Lord provided wonderful fellowship, encouragement, and comfort!

That was the only time I heard a Christian broadcast during all my eight years in bonds. But it happened at precisely the hardest time, when my soul desperately needed spiritual strengthening. How thankful I was for that broadcast from South Korea and for the radio missionaries who made it possible! All of the hardships of camp life suddenly became easier to bear.

The duty officer greeted me amiably when I arrived at the control point one morning for my routine check-in.

"I have good news for you," he said. "No more red stripe."

After six months of night checks and running to the control point every two hours during the day, that certainly was welcome news.

"Thank you, citizen officer! This is so unexpected. Are you now convinced that I'm not planning to escape?"

Though no one else was around, the officer lowered his voice. "We all knew you had no intention of escaping," he whispered. "It wasn't the camp officials who gave you the red stripe. It was the authorities in Moscow. They don't like you!"

Life was easier without that red stripe. I felt as though I were already halfway to freedom! Years later, I learned that Christians in my country and around the world had prayed for me and petitioned the Soviet government on my behalf. How thankful I am that they remembered the prisoners, including me.

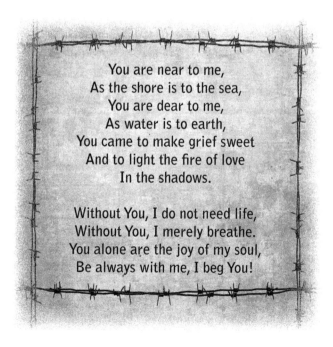

You are near to me,
As the shore is to the sea,
You are dear to me,
As water is to earth,
You came to make grief sweet
And to light the fire of love
In the shadows.

Without You, I do not need life,
Without You, I merely breathe.
You alone are the joy of my soul,
Be always with me, I beg You!

7

THE GREAT ESCAPE TUNNEL

The camp at Tabaga was surrounded by four thick, wooden stockade-like fences nearly fifteen feet high. Over each fence stretched several rows of barbed wire and another wire connected to the alarm system. Massive spirals of barbed wire lay between the first two fences. Armed guards with dogs patrolled the area between the last set of fences. If the alarm was triggered, a piercing screech would rip through the air and a flashing red light at the control point pinpointed where the alarm was set off, sending soldiers rushing to the location.

Most of the violators of the forbidden zones turned out to be stray cats and wild animals. But early one morning, a guard dog discovered a tunnel under the fence leading from the camp to freedom. Someone was preparing to escape!

The alarm went off. Soldiers rushed about. The prisoners were hurried from their work places to the open square in the center of the camp where attendance was taken. As usual, the number of prisoners present did not correspond with the number on the list. We were counted two more times before the numbers matched. No one had escaped.

That left camp authorities with the problem of finding out just who was preparing to escape. About thirty soldiers and officers faced the prisoners. They brought the dog that had discovered the tunnel. It was a large, fierce German shepherd trained to hate prisoners. At the sight of a man in a prisoner's uniform, the animal's hackles would rise and a deep-throated snarl curled its lips to reveal rows of gleaming teeth.

"Attention, citizen prisoners! An escape tunnel has been discovered!" the colonel announced. "Who prepared it? It will be better for you to speak up now. The dog will find you out in any case." He pointed to the dog straining at its leash toward the prisoners. "Whoever dug the tunnel, three steps forward!"

Nobody moved. The colonel swore.

"Ha! You're all scared! You're not afraid to cause trouble, but you're too cowardly to own up to it. Count off by threes!" he ordered.

One, two three, one, two, three. The numbers rang out.

"Every third one, move five steps forward," commanded the colonel, thrusting his arm skyward.

A third of the prisoners moved forward five steps and froze. Victor was among them. An officer gave the dog an object to sniff, then released it among the prisoners.

The dog lunged toward the nearest prisoner who cried out with terror and pain as fangs pierced his flesh. With lightning speed, the dog grabbed for a second, then a third prisoner.

It was a nightmare. Prisoners screamed and shouted as the animal tore into them. The officers grouped together nearby to observe, chuckling maliciously. I saw Victor grimace in pain as he grabbed his leg where the dog bit him. Silently, I called out to the Lord to protect us.

As the dog lunged toward yet another prisoner, the man turned quickly and kicked the animal's head with his heavy boot. The dog squealed in surprise and tucked its tail between quivering legs.

"What are you doing?" shouted an officer. "Don't hurt that dog! We'll punish you!"

But now the prisoners couldn't be stopped. Some tried to get the dog. Others shouted. A soldier finally managed to grab the cowering creature and protect it from the prisoners. Order was soon restored and we were sent to our barracks. The dog's victims received no medical attention for their wounds.

The next day it was determined that the "escape tunnel" was nothing more than the burrow of a wild animal! Closer examination revealed that, though the hole was wide, only a small child could have fit through it, certainly not a grown man.

Of course there were attempts to escape, but they were mostly unsuccessful. Thomas, who was about thirty-five years old, had been a prisoner for ten years already but could no longer stand the brutal conditions of slavery. In broad daylight, he scaled the first fifteen-foot fence just outside the work zone. The alarm malfunctioned, failing to alert the soldiers to the escape. Silent prisoners watched in fascinated horror as Thomas methodically picked his way through the masses of barbed wire and over the remaining three fences. Once out of the

SOVIET PRISON CAMP SOLIDIERS WITH THEIR DOGS

camp, Thomas walked slowly toward the river. He had gone about 200 yards before the soldiers set off in pursuit. They shouted to him, but he didn't stop or even turn around. The soldiers opened fire and filled his back with bullets. No one will ever know what Thomas was thinking during his reckless act. Perhaps he was searching for death.

If a prisoner died at camp, a military doctor issued the death certificate. But even that didn't completely satisfy the camp administration. Only after officers personally verified that the prisoner was, in fact, dead, was the body carried to the control point in a simple wooden box. There, in the presence of at least two officers, the lid was opened and guards stabbed the body several times with a bayonet. After this, the dead prisoner was "released" from the camp.

In Stalin's time, the gruesome procedure was much simpler. Soldiers would break the skull of the corpse with an iron hammer, then throw the naked body into a common grave without any kind of casket.

At Tabaga, we had a middle-aged prisoner nicknamed "Chuma," the Plague. He got the name because of the filthy job he had oiling equipment at the camp. His clothes were always dirty, torn, and stained with a dark, foul-smelling liquid. His prison career had begun when Stalin was in power. Over the years, he had been released several times but was always rearrested. Sometimes we talked about the concentration camps under Stalin in the territories of Kolyma and Yakutia.

"Petrovich,"—like many prisoners, Chuma addressed me by my patronymic—"if an investigative commission came to the North now to investigate the burial places of prisoners, I could show them hundreds of common graves where thousands of our fellow prisoners are buried. And I tell you, those corpses are intact and well preserved. The permafrost is an eternal freezer!"

"Weren't they buried in caskets?" I asked.

Chuma laughed. "Are you so naive? Hundreds died every day. Where would they get that many caskets? And they buried the dead naked. Clothing was scarce here in the North. Why waste it? A little piece of wood with the prisoner's number was tied to the big toe of the right foot. That's all. So they lie there, even now, piled up. Thousands in each hole."

"Somewhere in such an unknown grave in the North lies my father's body," I said. "He died of starvation in 1943 at a camp in Kolyma not far from Magadan." And I told Chuma about my father and the thousands of other Christians tormented to death in concentration camps because of their faith.

By the time I was a prisoner, most camps in the North had cemeteries. The wooden box containing the body was carried to a grave dug just outside the fences. The lid would be opened in the presence of an officer and a metal plate with the prisoner's number was laid on his chest. Then the lid was nailed shut and the box lowered into the hole. A metal bar also showing the prisoner's number, not his name, was pounded into the ground to mark the spot. Family members of the deceased were permitted to visit the grave site, but they could not move the body to a cemetery in their hometown until the prison term that was being served actually ended.

Tabaga's cemetery was on a nearby hill covered with scrubby pine trees. An officer often pointed that hill out to me. "When your ten-year term is up," he'd say, "you'll get another ten years. We'll keep that up until you die. Deny God, and you can go home now!"

But other, quite different words echoed in my heart:

Whosoever therefore shall confess me before men, him will I confess also before my Father which is in heaven. (Matthew 10:32)

Oh, Jesus, help me to remain faithful to You to the end!

IN PRISON UNIFORM

8

GRANDPA VASILY'S STORY

Half of Tabaga's prisoners were Yakuts, a northern people. Though only about 300,000 in number, the Yakuts occupy a territory nearly as large as all of Western Europe. Traditionally, Yakuts are hunters, fishermen, and reindeer herders whose ancestors came from the South near China. They have dark, slanted eyes, coal-black hair, and high cheekbones.

The Yakutian capital was founded by Russians in 1638, and today about 300,000 to 400,000 Russians live in this territory. Before the 1917 Revolution, several hundred Russian Orthodox churches and priests were scattered throughout Yakutia. Fewer than ten Russian Orthodox churches survived.

At Tabaga I met an elderly Yakut nicknamed "Grandpa Vasily." He was tall and thin with a long narrow face and a sparse white beard. He was kind and friendly, but he loved vodka. Because of it he had already been imprisoned several times. After drinking even a little, Grandpa Vasily completely lost control, getting into fights and even committing murder.

"I know that you're here because of your Christian faith and the Gospel," Grandpa Vasily said, peering at me kindly with his narrow eyes. "Faith in God is a very good thing. A lot of people in my village used to believe in God and go to church. But now we don't have any churches. All of them were destroyed, and our people started drinking vodka. I'm such a sinner! I love vodka with a passion!" He spat on the ground in annoyance at himself. "And because of that cursed bottle I'm in camp for the third time. I don't even know why I love vodka so much, more than I love my wife, my children, and my grandchildren. When I was free, I couldn't live a day without vodka. Here I go without it for years."

"Do you believe in God?" I asked.

"Of course! Yakuts are Orthodox Christians! It's just that when the authorities took God from us, our lives were turned upside down." Moving closer, he whispered in my ear, "I was an official in our village, but I drank everything away! And now everybody in our village drinks, men and women alike. Vodka is all people talk about. Instead of bowing to God, we Yakuts bow before our vodka. If you want, I'll tell you how it all started."

And Grandpa Vasily told me his story.

"Right after the Revolution, the church in our village was closed. The authorities put a big lock on the door and sent our priest to a concentration camp. He was a kind man, and everyone respected him. Very few people were literate then, and everyone asked the priest to read and write letters for them. He also counseled them on family matters. After the priest was arrested, his wife and children were exiled. No one in our village ever heard of them again."

Grandpa Vasily shook his head in painful remembrance, then continued his tale.

"One day some officials from the nearest town came to our village. They tried to open the lock on the church door. When they couldn't get it open, they just broke down the door. Then they took all of the religious books, Bibles, and New Testaments and piled them in the town square. Anything pertaining to God was declared harmful and had to be destroyed. The books were set ablaze while the officials joined hands and danced around the fire, laughing like madmen. The horrified Orthodox believers stood nearby, watching the whole thing. I was just twelve years old then."

Grandpa Vasily's parents, who were Orthodox, were very upset by what they saw. Young Vasily could no longer stand by in shocked silence. Darting up to the flaming pile, he snatched one of the burning books and disappeared into the forest. People began yelling. Someone ran after him but couldn't find him.

Vasily got home late that night. He and his parents examined the book he had rescued from the fire. The beautiful leather binding had suffered little damage. Vasily's parents couldn't read, but with great reverence, they slowly turned the pages. Then they wrapped it in clean white linen and hid it.

Grandpa Vasily shook his head mournfully. "All of our religious books were burned in that fire. The believers salvaged what small portions they could and kept them as holy relics. The cross was torn off the church, and the building was used as a storage shed for a collective farm until it was eventually demolished."

"What happened to your Bible?" I asked.

"My father kept it for many years. Then he gave it away."

"Did you ever read it?" I wondered.

"No," he sighed. "It was written in Old Church Slavonic, a language I don't understand. How I would love to read the Gospel!" Grandpa Vasily lowered his voice. "Do you have a Gospel here in camp?"

"No, not yet. But when I get one, I'll let you read it," I promised.

Many prisoners came to me with the same request. We really needed a Gospel, and so I began to pray more earnestly about it.

> No! You cannot kill the freedom of belief,
> Or shut Christ up in jail!
> The examples of His triumphs
> Will live in hearts He's saved.

1968—GEORGI'S WIFE, NADIA (CENTER) WITH CHILDREN BEFORE TRAV-
ELING TO VISIT GEORGI IN PRISON IN URAL MOUNTAINS: NATASHA (TOP
LEFT), PETER (FAR RIGHT), LISA (FRONT), JANE (HELD BY MOTHER)

9

MAMA'S VISIT

y mother wanted to visit me. For a prisoner, the anticipation of seeing relatives is a source of unending joy. Prisoners will talk about an upcoming meeting for months in advance. "Soon my wife and children will come to visit me!" or "Soon my Mama will be here! She promised to come see me!"

This is especially true if you're a Christian prisoner. Although you've been wrenched from your family and church, your heart remains with God's people in freedom. Not even prison can separate you from believers or deprive you of the ministry entrusted to you by God, and you understand very well what Paul wrote in his letter to the Philippians: "Even as it is meet for me to think this of you all, because I have you in my heart; inasmuch as both in my bonds, and in the defense and confirmation of the gospel, ye all are partakers of my grace. For God is my record, how greatly I long after you all in the bowels of Jesus Christ" (Philippians 1:7, 8). The words of Jesus Christ are also precious to you: "I am the good shepherd: the good shepherd giveth his life for the sheep. But he that is an hireling, and not the shepherd, whose own the sheep are not, seeth the wolf coming and leaveth the sheep, and fleeth: and the wolf catcheth them, and scattereth the sheep" (John 10:11, 12). Even if you're in prison many years, you constantly pray for each member of your church.

There's very little you can say in a letter because all letters are censored. But when your family comes, they give you the latest news about your church and friends. That's why the Christian is so excited about the upcoming visit.

The journey from my home in Kiev to the prison camp in Yakutsk is almost 4000 miles by air. Traveling by train and car stretches the distance to over 6000 miles. My mother made the trip with my oldest son Peter. We were allowed only a short meeting in the presence of an officer. The officer also watched as a guard frisked me before the meeting.

"You are permitted a four-hour meeting," the officer said. "You will sit behind one table, your mother and son will sit behind another table. There are to be no letters, no notes, and no instructions for the church. You are not permitted to speak about the conditions in camp. If any of these rules are broken, the meeting will come to an abrupt end."

As I entered the room, my mother stood up. The officer stopped her: "Citizen! It is forbidden to approach a prisoner!"

"But I'm his mother!" she objected. "I want to embrace my son!"

"It is forbidden! You've been warned!" the officer shouted.

Mama returned to her seat next to Peter at the table. The officer pointed to the opposite table. Before sitting down I asked, "Citizen officer, we are Christians. We cannot begin our meeting without praying. Please allow us to pray."

"Well, praying is forbidden here," he said doubtfully. He threw his hands up in resignation. "But I'll make an exception. Go ahead and pray—but keep it short!"

I looked at my mother. "Mama, you pray. I need your blessing." We stood while she prayed.

How Mama had changed since I'd last seen her! So many new wrinkles had appeared on her face! And what sadness was concealed behind her eyes. She herself had only recently been released from a three- year term of imprisonment. Shortly after that, I was arrested and so for all those years we hadn't seen each other except for a few minutes at the prison in Kiev after my trial.

And Peter! He was already nineteen, tall, straight, and smiling. (I'd named him after my father who was uncompromising in his service to the Lord.) I was so glad that he came with his grandmother to see me in Tabaga.

Mama told me about my family and how the children missed me.

"Mama," I asked, "how is your health? How did you make it through those years in prison?"

"You can see I survived!" she smiled. "But when I got out, I could hardly walk. I was so weak that some of the guards had to hold me up and lead me by the arm out of the camp."

"You made this whole trip on your own, Babushka!" Peter exclaimed. "You hardly leaned on me at all, just when we were boarding the plane."

Mama asked about my health and if letters from the family were getting through. Then she said, "Even though things might get really hard, never get discouraged. The Lord is always with you. My prayers are constantly with you. Remain faithful to the Lord always, in everything. Be faithful until death!"

The officer seated between our tables became uncomfortable. "Don't talk about death! You're not supposed to prepare him for death!"

Peter told me about his study plans and about his little brother Alex. "He's getting so big! He's so full of life, so curious! Oh, if only you could see him!"

The time flew. "Oh!" Mama suddenly remembered, "I've got some food for you!" She turned to the officer. "Let me give him something to eat," she said, showing him the bag she'd brought.

"It's forbidden! He's not entitled to it!" he answered sharply.

"Just one little sausage sandwich!" she pleaded.

"I said no!" The officer was getting irritated.

The door of our meeting room opened into the corridor. Major Chetveryak, the assistant director of camp discipline, appeared in the doorway. "How's the meeting going?" he asked the officer.

"Everything's in order," he replied.

Mama jumped up and turned to Major Chetveryak. In her hand, she clutched a small Gospel. "Comrade Major, I brought my son a Gospel. Let me give it to him."

"A Gospel?" he exclaimed. "I can't allow that!"

"Oh, please! Just this once! There's nothing criminal in this book." Mama handed the Gospel to the major and he began paging through it. Mama pulled a sheet of paper out of her purse. "This is a petition that I wrote to the camp director asking permission for my son to have a Gospel," she said, handing the petition to the major.

He read it slowly. "You write here that the Gospel is not officially forbidden in our country. But this Gospel talks about God and we're building a society without religion. What can I do? The Bible contradicts our Soviet society and the policies of the Communist Party."

"But what about the Constitution?" Mama persisted.

"The Constitution and real life—those are two different things." (How well the major had summarized it!) "I'll take this Gospel and your petition. In a week I'll let your son know what is decided after I talk with the camp director." He put the book in his pocket.

"I have one more request," Mama said. "I brought something for my son to eat." She showed him her bag of food.

"He's not allowed to have food parcels until halfway through his sentence," interrupted the first officer.

But Mama wasn't giving up. "All I have is some bread, cheese, milk, and a little sausage. He could eat it right here," she pleaded, turning again to the major.

"Oh, all right," the major agreed. Then to the officer he added, "Just watch and make sure what kind of food it is."

Out of her bag, Mama pulled two hard boiled eggs, a hunk of white bread, some sausage, cheese, a small bottle of milk, a glass, and a white linen napkin.

The officer carefully examined everything. "Yes, you can give it to him."

Mama unfolded the napkin and placed it neatly before me on

the rusty black table before setting out the food. I prayed and began to eat slowly, savoring each bite. I hadn't eaten anything like it in over a year. How good it was to taste milk and fresh bread again! Mama beamed.

The officer glanced at his watch. "This meeting will end in fifteen minutes."

Again, I asked permission to pray. Then we had to part.

"Good-bye, Mama."

"Good-bye, son. The Lord be with you."

"Peter, remember that you have the name of your grandfather, who loved the Lord and the Russian people and was faithful to God until the end. I pray for you, my son, that you will give your heart to the Lord."

Mama and Peter were escorted from the room first. I just sat there, deeply moved by our meeting. I prayed silently until the officer returned for me. After another frisk, I was allowed back into the camp.

A week later, I asked Major Chetveryak about the Gospel.

"This matter has not been decided," he answered curtly.

A month later, the same words were repeated. I wrote a petition to the camp director requesting the Gospel. Major Chetveryak called me to his office.

"Your Gospel is in my safe," he said. "I won't give it to you in the camp. You'll get it back when you're released."

I never saw it again.

> By faith Moses, when he was come to years, refused to be called the son of Pharaoh's daughter; choosing rather to suffer affliction with the people of God, than to enjoy the pleasures of sin for a season; esteeming the reproach of Christ greater riches than the treasures in Egypt: for he had respect unto the recompence of the reward. (Hebrews 11:24-26) (favorite verses of Peter Vins, Georgi's father, who died in a Soviet prison at 39 years old)

LYDIA VINS (GEORGI'S MOTHER)
IMPRISONED FOR THREE YEARS FOR HER FAITH IN CHRIST

MY MOTHER'S IMPRISONMENT
"She hath done what she could." (Mark 14:8)

On December 1, 1970, my 63-year-old mother was arrested in Kiev. It happened in the evening. She was in the house with my youngest children.

After she had dressed and got ready, my elest daughter, Natasha, came home. Their grandmother was very calm and peaceful.

She prayed with her grandchildren and left the house accompanied by the policemen.

The first snow had fallen, forming a soft carpet over the earth, earth so rich in tears and sorrow.

The tall pine forest mother loved so much, which came right up to the town, looked down pensively upon the bustling people in miltary uniform, helping the old woman into the "black raven." Her beloved forest bade her farewell . . .

The children ran out into the streets without their coats and cried quietly.

10

HIDDEN TREASURES

Several months after my mother came, according to the camp schedule, I was due for a long visit with my family. We could be together for three days. How I looked forward to that meeting!

"I'm sure your family will bring you a Gospel," Victor said, "so we'd better be prepared. Let's make a hole for it in your boot."

Victor secretly removed the thick heels from my boots and carefully carved a hole in them with a knife. Then he pounded them back onto the boots.

Our plan was for me to wear the boots to my meeting. If my family brought a complete New Testament, I would tear out the Gospel of John and hide eleven chapters in one heel and ten in the other.

The evening before the meeting with my family was scheduled to begin, a guard told me that they'd arrived. It was hard to fall asleep that night. I kept thinking about my wife Nadia and the children. My youngest son, Alex, was three now. The last time I saw him he was a one-year-old baby. Of course, he wouldn't remember me. I tried to imagine how much he had grown. My youngest daughter Jane would be ten, Lisa would be fourteen, Peter was nineteen, and my oldest daughter Natasha would be twenty-two. Oh, how little I had seen them these past few years! And Nadia—how was she getting along without me? Which of the children had come? I wondered. I wouldn't know until the next day. I prayed again and finally fell asleep.

In the morning, I learned that we would be allotted the full three days' visit. But even though the room was ready and the meeting scheduled, I was not permitted to see my family that day. I knew why. The same thing had happened during my first imprisonment in the Urals. My family would come for our meeting and even though the room was prepared, camp officials would delay the visit for a day or two, almost as though they were waiting for someone. And sure enough, a group of KGB agents would arrive laden with various equipment so they could secretly monitor our conversations. The KGB listened only to the conversations of Christians. They weren't concerned with the criminal prisoners. They were especially interested in matters like church morale.

After two long days, I was finally summoned for the meeting. In the search room, I was ordered to remove all my clothes, and even my boots. A soldier examined each article of clothing as two officers watched. One was a KGB worker. Tall, thin, with piercing eyes and a little mustache, he was a new officer wearing a crisp new uniform and black boots polished to gleaming perfection. His dark hair was slicked back and he reeked of cologne. He smiled as he watched, holding his cap in his hands. Everything about him, from his smile and the expression in his eyes down to his shiny boots, revealed a man very satisfied with himself and enjoying his new authority.

"What do you have that's forbidden?" he asked.

"What do you mean?"

"Letters or instructions for your church."

"You're mistaken, citizen officer. The church does not need instructions from me. The church gets instructions from God in the Bible. And God Himself engraves them on the heart of every believer," I replied calmly.

"Ha!" the officer sneered. "Look where your faith has brought you! You're nothing but a criminal!" He picked up one of my boots, holding it at arm's length. Then he set it on the table and began checking it.

My heart skipped a beat. Even though nothing was hidden in the heel, I knew that the entire meeting would be cancelled if the holes in the heels were discovered!

But Victor had done his work well and the officer put the boot back on the shelf. He didn't even look at the other boot. I was ordered to get dressed and the officers left me with the guards. As I dressed, another officer entered the room, the one who had allowed me to listen to a Christian radio broadcast in the middle of the night. He looked at me and smiled.

"What are they searching for? Your faith? Your faith isn't in your pocket, it's in your soul! You can't hide it. Let's go to your meeting. Your family has been waiting in the room for two hours already. They passed the search. You Christians don't drink vodka or use drugs. If it was up to me, I wouldn't bother frisking Christians."

After the guards walked on ahead, he closed the door and whispered, "If I were in power, I'd let all you Christians go home free!"

The officer led me down the corridors of the administration building back to the control point and from there down another long, narrow hall to the room for our meeting. He inserted a key into the lock and the door swung open. Then I saw the beautiful smiles of my beloved wife and all five children! They surrounded me, the younger ones jumping up and down in their excitement, all talking at once. What great joy! For several years, I'd dreamed of being with my family, of seeing the dear faces of those I loved best, hugging them, hearing their happy voices.

After everyone calmed down, I noticed my little Alex standing to one side, watching me shyly. I held out my hand. "Hello, Alex."

Without a word, he ran to his mother and hid his face in her skirt. Although he knew I was his father, I was still a stranger. One of his sisters began coaxing him. "Come on, this is your Papa! Don't be shy!"

But the coaxing made him even more timid.

"Let him be," I said. "He'll get used to me soon and everything will be fine. Right now let's pray and thank the Lord for this meeting."

We knelt and gave thanks to God. We knew that the KGB was

recording every word we spoke and that later in Moscow the tapes would be reviewed and analyzed to refine their strategy for the battle against the church. But there on our knees we didn't think about the listening devices. Only the Lord and our prayers to Him were reality at that moment. I listened to the prayers of my children thanking God for the opportunity to see their Papa. And my wife, after years of separation from me, was giving thanks to God for His leading and tender care.

We talked for hours. But because we couldn't speak freely about everything, Nadia had brought paper, pencils, and matches. The most important messages were written on paper, then burned and the ashes thrown in the toilet.

The first message was, "We brought you a Gospel. It wasn't discovered during the search. We also have a camera, but it's in the village at someone's apartment where we left the rest of our things."

I was glad to see that Alex was getting used to me. At first, he wouldn't talk directly to me. He'd go to one of his sisters, whisper in her ear and say, "Tell that to him!" But by the second day, he would look right at me and say, "Papa, play with me!" or "Papa, tell me a story!" Finally, he announced to his sisters, "Now I know I have a Papa, too!"

And I found out about his trip to visit me. On the bus going to the airport in Moscow, Alex met a little girl his age whose name was Tanya. "Are you going to prison to see your Papa, too?" Alex asked suddenly.

A hush settled over the bus as everyone stared at Alex. He continued his little speech. "I'll see my Papa soon. He lives in prison. And we'll bring him home. Papa's prison is in the North, and it's very cold there."

Fortunately, my wife restrained him from elaborating any further on his story. Tanya's mother pulled her onto her lap, faced her toward the window, and looked the other way.

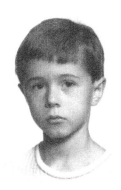

ALEX

Alex didn't understand her reaction. Since his father was in prison, it only made sense that other children's fathers probably were, too.

There was so much to talk about! The children were growing. Each one was a fresh, lively world of aspirations and problems, an unending stream of conversation. I made time to speak with each one individually, to find out more about their lives and to try to answer hundreds of questions. Then suddenly the words would stop and a finger would fly to our lips in warning. "Quiet! We can't talk about this openly!" And the rest of the conversation would continue with paper and pencil.

Using notes, my family told me that the church was doing well, that Christians were cheerful and alert, and that the Lord was blessing the ministry. They told me of people getting saved, people being baptized, and of teenagers and children filling the services. They told me about the Christian Publishing House and the New Testaments, hymn books, and other Christian literature being printed secretly in Russian, Ukrainian, and some of the other languages spoken in our country. My daughter Natasha told me in a note, "We're expecting soon to publish the whole Bible in Russian!" I thought back to March 1974 when I was arrested while carrying the microfilm that was to be used to prepare the printing plates. How I worried when it was confiscated. Now they would go ahead with the printing! Praise the Lord!

My family wanted to know details of my life in camp. I spoke openly about conditions, but never mentioned the names of people to whom I was witnessing.

Mealtimes were especially lively. My family had brought meat, potatoes, and fresh vegetables—food unheard of in Tabaga. They even brought oranges! That was a very special treat, not only in the North but at home in Kiev as well. The youngest children kept looking at those oranges, touching them with their little fingers. I really loved peeling the oranges, smelling the skin, and watching my children eat them. At first, Alex pushed away my hand holding a peeled orange out to him and said, "Eat it yourself."

"You eat it, Alex," I urged. "Onions and garlic taste better to me than oranges!"

So he held out his little hand waiting for his piece of orange, convinced that I just wasn't interested in them.

It really was the garlic and onions that I loved. I kept eating them with the fresh Ukrainian bread. I couldn't get enough!

The next day an officer came to the meeting room and announced to my wife, "The camp director wants to see you in his office."

How odd. Was our meeting going to be interrupted? We prayed before my wife left the room. She took along an empty bottle so that as long as she was away, she could look for milk. When she returned two hours later, the bottle was filled with fresh milk.

"Who was it? What did they want?" The children and I were anxious to know.

"Drink the milk," she instructed the children. I, too, enjoyed a glass of milk.

Nadia took a sheet of paper and started writing. "The camp director and a KGB officer talked with me. They said, 'It must be hard for you and your children to be without their father. We are willing to let him go home with you if he will write a statement renouncing all of his criminal religious activities and if he promises to reform his old way of life.'"

"And what did you say?" I asked. "Tell me out loud."

Nadia cleared her throat. "I asked the camp director if he had talked with you about this. He said, 'Yes, but he refuses to write such a statement. Perhaps you can convince him because you're the mother of his children. Think of your poor children growing up without their father.'

"Then the KGB officer said, 'If he won't write the statement, you can write it for him. Write a letter to the authorities asking for mercy. Say that you'll do everything in your power to keep him from committing more crimes.' I said, 'My husband has never committed a crime. He is a Gospel preacher and he'll never renounce that ministry.' The KGB officer said, 'Your husband has been sentenced to ten years. When that term is up, he'll get another ten years. So think about that for a while.'

"Then, with honey dripping from his voice, the camp director said, 'Oh, yes, think it over. Don't hurry home. Stay a few days. We could call a commission to settle this matter and in a few days, your husband could go home with you. Wouldn't that be nice? Just two or three days and he'd be a free man again! Here's some paper. Start writing."

Nadia and I both knew that there could be only one response.

I spoke loudly and distinctly so that those monitoring our conversations would be sure to hear each word. "I'll never stop preaching the Gospel as long as I live. And I'll never betray the persecuted church.

That would be the same as betraying Jesus Christ." Then the whole family knelt and we took turns praying aloud, asking the Lord to help us remain faithful to the end.

After her meeting with the camp director, Nadia had gone to the village where she and the children had left their belongings. She bought some milk and hid a small camera under her coat. This time she was not searched before entering the meeting room. As we did every evening, we pulled the shades down over the window. Then Peter took several photographs of us.

That evening I hid the Gospel of John in my boot heels. Using a dinner knife, I very carefully pried the heels off the boots. I tore out eleven chapters from John's Gospel, folded them into quarters, and tried to insert them into the hole. They wouldn't fit. Just eight chapters could go in that hole and only seven into the other. Then I beat the heels back into place with the knife. The children made a point of having a lot of noisy fun as I worked so that the pounding wouldn't be heard.

I'd just finished replacing the boot heels when my family surprised me with a tiny Gospel of Mark! Several thousand mini-Gospels had been printed secretly by the Christian Publishing House right there in the Soviet Union, a special edition intended for Christian prisoners. I recalled how I had prayed with a printing team as we discussed printing those tiny Gospels. There I was, a prisoner myself, holding one in the palm of my hand.

But how would I get this treasure into the camp? Nothing more could fit into the boot heels. After thinking it over, I decided to sew the Gospel into the hem of my undershirt. Then I put it on and took it off without letting go of the part with the Gospel sewn in. Nadia and the children watched closely as I repeated the maneuver. They didn't notice anything either in my hand or sewn into the shirt. I practiced several more times to be sure.

The three days passed quickly. Before we knew it, soldiers stood at the door, hurrying me along. It was so hard to part! Little Alex flung his arms around my neck. "Papa, come with us!" he cried. "I can't go home without you!" I held him close.

Nadia was weeping and my daughters were wiping tears from their eyes. Tears welled up inside me as well. But I had to be strong. The children mustn't see me cry.

Setting Alex back on the floor, I spoke to him as to a man. "Alex, I must stay here at the camp because I haven't finished the work the Lord has given me. I'm a Gospel preacher, and thousands of prisoners here have never heard about Jesus. God has given me a very important assignment. My little son let me stay here, just a little while longer."

That little boy had learned a lot during those days at camp. By speaking to him seriously and calmly, I was able to settle him down. The guards waited as I prayed with my family one last time. I embraced each one and said good-bye. They watched as the guards led me away. We knew at least a year would pass before we saw each other again.

How long wilt thou forget me, O Lord? for ever? how long wilt thou hide thy face from me? How long shall I take counsel in my soul, having sorrow in my heart daily? how long shall mine enemy be exalted over me? Consider and hear me, O Lord my God: lighten mine eyes, lest I sleep the sleep of death; Lest mine enemy say, I have prevailed against him; and those that trouble me rejoice when I am moved. But I have trusted in thy mercy; my heart shall rejoice in thy salvation. I will sing unto the Lord, because he hath dealt bountifully with me. (Psalm 13:1-6)

In the search room, I was ordered to empty my pockets. I took out my treasures—several large heads of garlic.

"This is forbidden!"

"This isn't meat, butter, or sugar. These are like vitamins! It's our medicine against scurvy. Please consider the garlic as medicine," I pleaded.

"No! It's forbidden!" They took away my garlic and ordered me to strip. I took my clothes off and lifted my undershirt without removing it. The little Gospel was in my hand.

The soldier nodded. "You don't have to take that off." They went painstakingly through every seam and every pocket of my clothing—except the undershirt! My boots were also closely examined.

"Do you have money?" the soldier asked.

"No money."

"Drugs?"

"No drugs. I'm a believer. I have only my faith."

"That's your own business. Keep it to yourself. Get dressed."

The search was over. The Gospels were safe!

JANE AND ALEX WITH THEIR IMPRISONED FATHER DURING
A FAMILY MEETING IN 1976 AT THE YAKUTSK PRISON CAMP

TABAGA, SIBERIA, WHERE GEORGI WAS IMPRISONED FOR FOUR YEARS (1975-1979)

11

A GIFT FOR GRANDPA SHAKY

As soon as I got back inside the prisoner zone, I saw Victor. "How did things go?" he asked.

"Everything got through!" He was amazed when I showed him the tiny Gospel of Mark.

Later Victor got my boots, removed the heels, and took out the precious chapters from the Gospel of John. Even though it was only a few hundred yards from the meeting room back to the barracks, several pages were crumpled and some words were rubbed off. But Victor managed to press the pages smooth and to tape most of them back together and he fashioned a pretty binding and cover. Right away he wanted to borrow the Gospel for his friend Mikhail.

Mikhail, about thirty years old, of medium height and stocky build, was a truck driver who loved to drink. One day he ran over a pedestrian. When the victim later died in the hospital, Mikhail was imprisoned. He left a wife and eight-year-old daughter behind.

Mikhail's wife was from a Christian family. As a child, she had gone to church and heard much about God. But as she grew older, she stopped going to church and began dating unsaved men. She was eighteen when she met and married Mikhail, a fun-loving man who liked to move with the fast crowd. Soon they had a daughter. The grandmother loved that little girl and took her home for weekend visits and spoke to the girl's parents about God.

"I got so tired of her talking about God, I didn't want to hear another word," Mikhail recalled. "I told my wife that our daughter shouldn't go visit anymore, and I wanted my wife to stop seeing her mother altogether."

But here was Mikhail, in a far northern camp, reading the Gospel for himself. Before I even arrived in that camp, Victor had been telling Mikhail about Jesus Christ and let him read his Gospel until it was confiscated. A fierce battle still raged in his soul. I was glad to hear that Mikhail's wife had begun attending Christian meetings and their little girl was living with her grandmother and going to church.

Two days after the meeting with my family, I was summoned to the control point.

"Did you have garlic with you after that meeting?" the officer on duty asked.

"Yes, but the soldiers took it from me."

"The camp director has permitted you to have it."

"Thank you!" Carefully I put five or six large heads of garlic into my jacket pocket. Oh, what riches! I was so thankful to the Lord for this gift.

Victor met me back at the barracks.

"Why were you called to the control point?" he asked anxiously.

"They returned my garlic," I answered, showing him our newest treasure.

"Time for a party!" he exclaimed.

I went to my bunk and addressed the prisoners around me. "I have some garlic. If you want some, come over here. If you have any bread, bring it."

About ten men surrounded me, including Victor and Mikhail. I opened an old newspaper onto my cot and pulled out the garlic. Pieces of black bread began to appear. Someone had some salt.

Before anyone took a bite, I said, "I got this garlic from my family. The soldiers took it during the strip search. But my God worked in the heart of the camp director, and now he has given this garlic back to me! So I want to pray and thank God for this precious gift."

I prayed aloud while the men waited. Then, how greedily

everyone attacked that garlic! They took little cloves and rubbed it on their pale, bleeding gums. They sprinkled their bread with salt and then rubbed garlic on it.

One head of garlic was still in my pocket. I was saving it for a certain old man in the camp. "Grandpa Shaky," as he was called, was around eighty years old. He was one of about twenty elderly prisoners in Tabaga, all over seventy-five. Some were still able to work. Grandpa Shaky was very weak and his hands shook all of the time. It was difficult for him to eat because he trembled so badly. But his legs were strong and he could walk to the mess hall. I never did know why Grandpa Shaky was in prison and he never said. He'd been in Tabaga for ten years and everyone knew him, prisoners and guards alike.

People often joked with him. "So when are you going home, Grandpa Shaky?" they'd ask. "When will you be free again?"

"In the year 2000," he'd solemnly answer.

I became friendly with Grandpa Shaky, whose real name was Ivan Vasilievich. I wanted to encourage him and tell him about Jesus Christ. He refused to hear a word about it.

"Georgi," he'd say, "thank you for being so kind to me, but don't talk to me about God. I don't believe in God and I don't want to hear anything about Him."

The next day I met him coming out of the mess hall. "How are you today, Ivan Vasilievich?"

"Still breathing," he answered as usual.

"I have some garlic for you," I said, holding out the treasure wrapped in newspaper.

"Oh, eat it yourself," he said. "You're still young. You need vegetables, especially garlic. I'm just an old man. I'll make it."

"Please take it," I urged. "You probably haven't seen garlic in a long time."

He paused and scratched his head. "Well, it's been about ten years since I've had any garlic or tomatoes or radishes. But somebody gave me an apple once."

"What about your family? Doesn't anybody come for visits?"

As soon as the words were out of my mouth, I realized I'd made a mistake.

Ivan Vasilievich's face darkened. "I don't have any family," he said angrily. "Nobody comes to see me and nobody's waiting for me even if I do get released." His hands trembled more than ever.

I pressed the garlic into his hand. "This is for you. You need it. Don't offend me by refusing. Please take it."

Tears rolled down his weathered cheeks. "Thank you, Georgi! This is the first time in ten years here!"

And with great difficulty, his shaky hands put that piece of garlic in his pocket and he walked slowly back to his barracks.

About a week later, I saw him again and he approached me smiling. "Greetings, Georgi! See, I'm still breathing! And now I smell like garlic when I breathe! I eat one clove a day. You know, I'm even feeling better. Did you notice my hands don't shake as much?"

"Yes, Ivan Vasilievich, and I see you're walking like a young man now!"

12

A HIGH-VOLTAGE READING ROOM

ach Sunday the prisoners got to see a film. Everybody looked forward to that big event. I didn't go to the movies, even though the camp administrator tried to force me. The captain in charge of my division was sent to discuss the matter with me.

"Why don't you go to the movies?" he asked. "They are a cultural, educational event and all prisoners are expected to attend."

"I'm a Christian," I answered. "I don't want to waste my time with meaningless films. You know I don't break camp rules and I do all my work. I'd go to the movies if you showed Christian films."

"Ha! That's all we'd need!" He was outraged. "We'll punish you for this! Everybody in the camp must view our Soviet films!" He ended the conversation.

Although I didn't actually go to the films, I looked forward to the movie hour each week because I could finally be alone in the quiet barracks. That was the best time to pray and read my little Gospel of Mark or the chapters of John. I was surrounded by silence. After days and nights of constant shouting, cursing, and fighting, at last I found blessed solitude. I read and wrote letters to my loved ones. I also prayed for the prisoners I saw every day. One of them was Yakov.

Yakov was serving the shortest sentence in camp. He was about twenty-eight years old, tall, thin, and very energetic. Everyone teased him because of his short term. "Oh, what a convict you are—sentenced to a whole year! You could stand that long on one leg!"

Yakov worked with me as an electrician. I found him to be quite sociable and very open to the message of salvation in Jesus Christ. He knew I had a little Gospel and really wanted to read it but not in the barracks for fear that the guards would catch him. So he asked if he could read it at work.

The factory was situated inside the camp limits, but far from the living zone, separated from it by a high fence. Several lumberyards were also within the camp confines. Huge electrical transformers stood near one of the lumberyards. Because it was a high-voltage area (10,000 volts), the transformers were surrounded by high wooden fences. A large red sign hung on the fence warning, "STOP! High Voltage!" The guards, soldiers, and officers were afraid of that area and seldom entered it. But we electricians occasionally went in to make a cautious inspection. In that danger zone, Yakov found a safe place for his quiet times. He showed me where he hid the Gospel so I could find it in case he got called to the control point and sent away to another camp.

Yakov loved to smoke. He said he'd been smoking for fifteen years. I didn't say anything to him about it, but one day, after reading the Gospel, he came to me and said, "I should really quit smoking. What do you think? Is smoking a sin?"

I explained that Christians don't smoke because nicotine is poison and harms your health.

Yakov began examining other areas of his life as well. He regretted that his lifestyle was so far from what the Gospel taught. Although still a young man, he had already been married three times.

"What have I done with my life?" he mourned. "I have three wives and four children waiting for me. Can God help me?"

We had a long talk about the Lord. Soon Yakov gave up smoking completely. He had quit smoking before but it never lasted more than a month. This time, though, Yakov was really disgusted with both the cigarettes and himself. He didn't give them away to his friends as he had in the past. He threw them on the ground and stomped on them.

But Yakov was wavering. Sometimes he would close up within himself. Then he'd go to the high-voltage area, isolate himself with the little Gospel and read, read, read.

Soon Yakov's year was up. Just before he was released, I gave him the address of some believers near his hometown in Siberia. I continued to pray that Yakov would give his heart to the Lord.

Meanwhile, the authorities were growing very concerned about my contact with Victor. One day the KGB conducted an unexpected search of our belongings. Every time the KGB workers walked past us, they'd stop us and check our pockets. We knew what they were looking for—our little Gospel! A lot of prisoners were reading God's Word and the authorities were uneasy.

One day after lunch, Victor was summoned to the control point and immediately sent to a camp 2000 miles from Tabaga. Mikhail had the little Gospel just then. Several weeks later, he received a letter from Victor. Victor couldn't write openly to me because of the censors. In his letter to Mikhail, he wrote, "Petrovich was a good example to me."

Coming from Victor, that little phrase really meant a lot to me. Although I never learned what became of him, I'm convinced that the Lord answered his aunt's prayers.

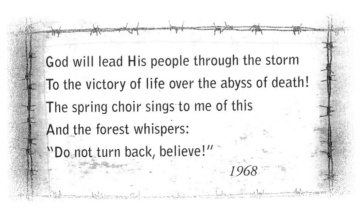

God will lead His people through the storm
To the victory of life over the abyss of death!
The spring choir sings to me of this
And the forest whispers:
"Do not turn back, believe!"
1968

1977—GEORGI, WITH HIS SON, PETER, WHO WAS VISITING
AT THE YAKUTSK PRISON CAMP IN SIBERIA

13

THE INVINCIBLE TRUTH

One Sunday evening I stepped out of the hot, stuffy barracks to get some fresh air. It was early October, but already a soft snow was falling. The recreation area where prisoners played volleyball in the summer was deserted. I walked back and forth across the playground, deep in thought, praying and singing a bit. After a while, I realized that I was not alone. Another prisoner was making his way toward me.

The stranger was a Yakut, about fifty years old, with broad shoulders and a stocky build.

"Are you Petrovich?" he asked in perfect Russian.

"Yes, that's what they call me," I answered. "Are you from the latest transport? I've never seen you before."

"I've been here two weeks already," he said with a grin. "My name is Stepan. May I talk with you? They tell me that you're a Christian, that you were arrested for your faith. I believe in God, too, but I was arrested for murder."

Then Stepan told me his story.

He was a mathematics teacher. He'd studied seven years at an institute in Leningrad specifically for the peoples of the North. Then Stepan returned to Yakutia and began teaching. He was arrested twice, both times for murder. His first prison term was ten years; this time he was sentenced to fifteen. He still had seven years to serve.

Stepan loved vodka. But he couldn't hold his liquor, and when he drank even a little, he would immediately lose control of himself. But now the Lord had begun to work in his heart.

Before coming to Tabaga, Stepan had been in a camp in the northern Urals. There he met a Christian prisoner who spoke a great deal about the Lord and was a good testimony. I was so glad that the seed of God's Word had already been sown in Stepan's heart, even though he'd never read or even seen a Gospel. As soon as Stepan found out that I was a Christian, he had decided to meet me.

"May I read your Gospel?" he asked. "Everyone knows you have one."

I gave Stepan the first fifteen chapters of the Gospel of John. He read them over and over. A week later, he asked if I had anything else. I held out the little Gospel of Mark.

"It's so tiny!" he exclaimed. "Are you sure it's a real Gospel?"

"Of course it's real! It's a mini-Gospel printed especially for prisoners," I explained.

After he had read that whole book through, he came to me and said, "Truth is defenseless, but it is invincible."

"What exactly do you mean by that?" I asked.

"Jesus Christ lived, was crucified, and died," Stepan said thoughtfully. "But He's alive today because He arose. And right now in our twentieth century, there are still Christians who love and believe Him and are willing to suffer for His teachings. That confirms that truth is invincible. The Gospel is alive! Jesus Christ cannot be destroyed! Faith in God is a great power! That's why I say that truth is defenseless but also invincible."

TO YOUNG CAPTAINS OF THE FAITH

For young captains of the faith,
On their way to Heaven,
I wish for faith without measure
And for courage to strengthen their hearts.

On the way will be winds of persecution,
A deceptive lull, like running aground,
Rocks of doubt underwater,
And the oppressive mist of unbelief.

But for those who are taught by Christ
To subdue the elements by strength of faith,
The sun of victory will shine
Through the gloomiest clouds.

At the sight of the wide sea
Of human tears and sorrows,
Do not desert people languishing in grief
Who have forgotten God!

Captains! Hold the banner higher!
The banner of God's radiant love!
Bring to life on the plains of humanity
The bright flame of the Good News.

For young captains of the faith,
On their way to Heaven,
I wish for faith without measure
And for courage to strengthen their hearts!

Anyusha Prison Camp
March 1969

GEORGI AS A YOUNG BOY WITH HIS FATHER, PETER VINS,
A FEW MONTHS BEFORE PETER'S FINAL ARREST

Two photos of Georgi's father, Peter,

Above: In Omsk prison in Siberia in 1937, right before Peter was executed at 39 years old;

Right: 1930 in Siberia

1955—KIEV, UKRAINE—GEORGI AND NADIA WITH NATASHA AND
GEORGI'S MOTHER, LYDIA

1958—GEORGI AND NADIA WITH NATASHA AND PETER

NATASHA WITH GRANDMOTHER LYDIA
AND GREAT-GRANDMOTHER MARIA

WHEN GEORGI WAS SENTENCED TO FIVE YEARS IN PRISON AND FIVE YEARS IN EXILE IN SIBERIA, THE CONFISCATION OF HIS PROPERTY WAS ALSO ORDERED.

ON THESE TWO PAGES, PHOTOS WERE CAPTURED OF THE VINS' FURNITURE
BEING REMOVED. LYDIA VINS AND OTHER FAMILY MEMBERS WERE PRESENT.
(USED WITH PERMISSION FROM KESTON INSTITUTE)

1972—Natasha (r.) with her friend, Inna, traveling to see grandmother Lydia who was in prison

1969—Georgi standing with son Peter after Georgi's release from one of his prison terms

14

ON THE PRISON TRAINS

The first half of my ten-year sentence was to end March 31, 1979. In late March, I was taken to the Yakutsk jail, where I spent a week in constant expectation, wondering where I would be sent for my exile.

One evening, when all thirty prisoners in that jail were lined up in the corridor for attendance, one of the officers recognized me.

"What are you doing here?" he asked.

"My five years of camp are over and I have five years of exile ahead of me. Do you know where they're sending me?"

He looked through my file. "Yes," he said. "You will be near Tyumen in western Siberia."

Late that evening we were loaded onto a police van and taken to the airport. A small plane was waiting for us and the guards. All prisoners were handcuffed. Each time the cold steel pinched my wrists, joy burst upon my heart: not for a crime or for any evildoing but for Christ my beloved Savior I found myself in these bonds again!

The propellers whirled as the engines revved up. The plane left the runway and headed south. Three hours later, we landed in Irkutsk. Then it was back to a police van, the prison, and searches.

Through it all the Lord continued to preserve my little Gospel of Mark.

I spent several days in the prison at Irkutsk waiting to continue my journey. The men I had been traveling with had already been shipped to other prisons.

A few days later, I boarded a Stolypin train car with other prisoners from Irkutsk. The Stolypin was like a miniature prison on wheels. It had about eight cells with wire mesh walls. Each cage was built to hold eight prisoners, but as many as twenty-five men were crammed into the compartments. Armed soldiers stood guard in the corridor.

PRISON IN IRKUTSK, EASTERN SIBERIA

Although we had been searched before boarding the train, we went through it again. As soon as the train was in motion, we were called out, three to five at a time, to wait in the corridor to be searched.

Just ahead of me stood a small, frail old man. He started to strip.

He tried to hurry but his hands trembled too badly. The soldiers yelled at him to move faster, which only made the old man more nervous. A soldier struck him with his fist. With a cry of pain, the old man slumped to the floor. There, with his shaky hands, he tried again to pull off his boots. Two young soldiers kicked him.

Being next in line, I saw everything. But what could I do? By Soviet law, I had no right to contradict a guard or even speak up for another prisoner. The young soldiers kept kicking that old man. My mind raced. *Should I keep silent? Look the other way? What about my Gospel? Maybe I'd have a better chance to preserve it if I said nothing.*

But what would Jesus do in my place? Would He be silent? Suddenly I spoke up. "What are you doing? Why are you beating him? He's old enough to be your grandfather! How can you treat someone like that?"

My reaction was so unexpected that even the guards were startled. Who was brazen enough to confront them? They stopped kicking the old man and turned to me.

"Don't you know the rules?" one of them yelled. "Nobody's bothering you!"

By now the old man had his boots off and was standing, but the soldiers had lost interest in him. "Get dressed!" they commanded.

One of them turned back to me. "Step up. Mr. Defender. Now it's your turn! We could put 'bracelets' on you, you know," he threatened.

The old man was taken back to his cage. I stripped quickly. One guard checked my clothing while the other went through everything in my bag. There he found a little box. He opened it. Inside was the tiny Gospel.

"What's this?" he asked with a sneer.

"It's the Gospel of Mark," I answered.

He started looking through it and then showed it to the other guard. "This is forbidden!" he announced and tossed it onto a pile of trash.

I immediately took the Gospel out of the garbage. "Throw it back!" shouted the soldier, his face flushed with rage.

"No!" I clutched it tightly in my palm.

The soldier forced my hand open and grabbed it. Holding it high over his head he started to tear it apart, sneering and mocking.

My mind raced. *Could I let him do that to God's Word? No!* I snatched the Gospel from his hands. "This is God's Word!" I said. "I won't let you tear it apart!"

The soldiers were furious. Such open defiance was unheard of! The soldiers had the right to handcuff, put into a straitjacket, or even execute any prisoner who defied their authority. They could have shot me on the spot.

The prisoners still waiting to be searched silently held their breath in fear and anticipation of the horror they were sure to witness.

"I'm going to make you tear up that book with your own hands!" one of the guards snarled. "Then I'll make you eat it!"

I gripped the little Gospel even tighter. "This book is my life!" I said, looking him straight in the eyes. "I'd rather be executed than tear it up!"

"This is my Gospel," I said, showing it to the officer. "It's my life, my faith! These soldiers wanted me to tear it up. I would never tear up this book."

The convoy officer heard the commotion and ran into the search room. "What's going on?"

The soldiers moved away from me and started to explain that I was being insubordinate and had almost started a riot against them. *How could I let the officer understand what was really happening?* Quickly I opened my hand.

"This is my Gospel," I said, showing it to the officer. "It's my life, my faith! These soldiers wanted me to tear it up. Because I believe in this book, I was sentenced to ten years in prison. I would never tear up this book."

"Give it to me," he said quietly.

I handed the tiny book to the officer and he left the car. The soldiers continued searching me.

"Now you're in for it!" one of them jeered. "He'll teach you how to fight for your 'rights'!"

My search was over and they went on to others. But I had to stand and wait for the officer. Everyone was certain that I would be severely punished because of that Gospel.

About ten minutes later, the officer returned. "This is your Gospel," he said. "You can keep it."

I thanked him. The soldiers looked confused. As I was taken back to my cage, the prisoners' hands started reaching out. "Show us the Gospel!" they cried. One of them asked me to read it out loud.

"Let me take a little break first," I answered. I closed my eyes and leaned back. *Oh, Lord, how I thank You for Your amazing intervention*, I prayed. Then I began reading the Gospel, first quietly and then louder and louder so that the prisoners in the next cell could hear about God's love. The soldier who had kicked the old man and threatened to tear up my Gospel stood nearby, listening silently.

I recalled Stepan's words: "Truth is defenseless, but it is also invincible." Not only had the Lord preserved the little Gospel of Mark, but He gave me an opportunity to openly proclaim its truth.

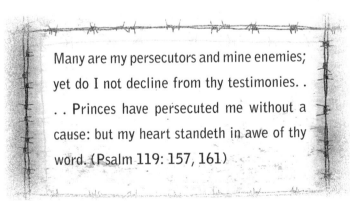

Many are my persecutors and mine enemies; yet do I not decline from thy testimonies. . . . Princes have persecuted me without a cause: but my heart standeth in awe of thy word. (Psalm 119: 157, 161)

ATHEISM'S WAR ON CHRIST'S TEACHINGS

Not so long ago, many people in our country supposed that there were almost no believers in the Soviet Union. By the 1960s, the voice of the Church had become very faint. Witness to Christ was bounded more and more by the walls of prayer houses, but inside these houses, the number of which has catastrophically decreased, ministers who had been false to God under the pressure of atheism led the task of curtailing the whole work of the Gospel. But here the Lord showed His mercy.

Atheism threw the entire state machine against the revived fellowship: the press, radio, television, police organs, procurators' offices, law courts, prisons, labor camps, and the Committee for State Security—the KGB.

However, the Lord gave His Church the strength to defend the work of evangelism. The whole country began to talk about the might of Christ and the power of His ideas.

Atheists try to distort the essence of Christ's teachings and slander His followers against their will, but the very fact of open, bitter war with God establishes a healthy concept in the consciousness of the Russian people: the matter concerns a living God, for one does not wage war with the dead!

—·—

..

15

THE MAN IN THE BLACK SWEATER

Late in the evening of our second day in transport the train rumbled into Novosibirsk. The prison car was disengaged from the rest of the train and dragged to a deserted dead end far from the bright lights and crowded station. Armed soldiers with guard dogs surrounded the train car. The soldiers kept their weapons pointed toward the prisoners. The large German shepherds barked wildly and strained at their leashes at the sight of the prisoners.

Each prisoner had to run quickly up a hill and across several railroad tracks into a waiting police van. Soldiers were yelling, trying to hurry the prisoners, who had to wait in line until the one ahead of him had entered the raven.

Then it was my turn. Guards shouted all around me as I ran, clutching my prison bag. Suddenly I tripped on one of the rails and fell flat. I couldn't catch my breath. More shouts and curses filled the air. A soldier uncoiled a few feet of leash, allowing his eager dog to come at me. Although restrained by a muzzle, gleaming teeth flashed in my face and I smelled the animal's hot, foul breath. I struggled to my feet and, accompanied by both dog and soldier, ran as fast as I could to the raven. Just as I reached it, the soldier released the dog which leaped into the van with me. Shouts of laughter and the frenzied barking of the dogs echoed in my ears.

We rode through the dark streets of Novosibirsk to the prison. "Home sweet home!" several of the prisoners said. "We'll finally get a good night's sleep before our next trip." We were exhausted because for two days and two nights we had neither slept nor eaten in that crowded prison train. But first we had to endure another search. This one took hours.

As I was searched, I prayed, *Oh, Lord, preserve my little Gospel and help me. I have no human strength left for a new battle.* Again, the Gospel remained safe!

We were taken to a long, dark corridor. Both walls were lined with heavy metal doors of prison cells. A row of dim electric lights suspended from the ceiling deepened the eerie atmosphere.

"Sit down!" a guard commanded.

A hundred prisoners quietly obeyed and sat on the cold cement floor. An officer called out the prisoners' last names. Guards escorted small groups of prisoners to their cells. An hour later, I was still sitting there. Before long, I was the only prisoner left.

At last, my name was called and I was led down the long corridor. I had been issued an old, dirty mattress and a lumpy, filthy pillow. In one arm, I held my bedding, in the other my bag of personal belongings. I was completely exhausted. My legs felt like dead weights. My mind couldn't accept anything more. All I could think about was lying down and sleeping, even right there on the cold cement floor.

Finally, the guard stopped, looked in the peephole of a heavy metal door, turned the key in the lock, and pushed the door open.

"Go in," he said, motioning me inside. The door closed and locked behind me. Heavy tobacco smoke hung in layers throughout the cell. Two electric bulbs burned dimly on the ceiling. The cell was not large, built to hold sixteen men. Metal bunk beds lined the walls. In the center of the room stood a wooden table and two wooden benches. A toilet and water faucet were partially hidden behind a short wall in the corner.

Although it was after midnight, none of the prisoners were asleep. They were upset about something and had been arguing among themselves. Some stood in the center of the cell near the door. Others sat at the table. A few lay on the bunk beds. Nearly everyone stared at me with hostility. Something about the atmosphere in the cell alarmed me.

"Good evening," I said, then corrected myself. "Good night." I dropped my mattress and pillow on the floor. "I haven't slept for two days. Just got off the transport train."

I started moving toward what looked like a vacant bunk, but two prisoners blocked my way.

"Why are you entering our 'home' so late?" asked a tall man in a black sweater.

"I just got off the transport," I answered.

"You were alone on a whole transport train?" a voice piped in from a bunk.

"No, there were about a hundred of us from the Irkutsk prison."

"Where are they? Why were you brought here alone? It's a trap!" someone shouted.

"Get out of here! Call a guard! We've seen people like you before!" growled the man in the black sweater. He pointed to the door.

I had no energy left to explain. "I just want to sleep," I said, trying to make peace. "I've gone two days and nights without sleep."

Several men began cursing me.

My spirit cried out to God. *Oh, Jesus, be with me! I don't even know where I am.*

A skinny little old man made his way out of the crowd. "How many people have you killed?" he rasped.

"I'm a Christian. I never killed anyone. I was sentenced twice for my faith in God," I answered.

"Where were you in prison before?"

"My first term was in the northern Urals. I just finished five years' strict regime in Yakutia."

"So you're a Christian and not a murderer?" the man in the black sweater asked. "First time I've met anyone like you in prison. Why were you put here in this cell? All of us are murderers." He pointed to the little old man. "And this one killed five people. We all just came from our trials and we're going to be sent to special strict-regime camps." He began cursing the judge and God.

"Why curse God?" I objected. "He didn't bring you here."

"We know your type," he shouted, moving toward me. "Get out of here! You're not a Christian!" He shoved me with his shoulder.

I didn't know what to do. The hostile faces of prisoners surrounded me. In my eight years of prison life, nothing like this had ever happened. Shouts, curses, threats, and an evil that I couldn't comprehend filled the cell.

"You say you're a Christian?" someone shouted. "Prove it! Let's see your Bible!" Others echoed the command.

My thoughts raced madly. *Should I show them my little Gospel of Mark? What if they tear it up? No, I must show it to them. The Lord will protect His Word from these murderers just as He protected it from the soldiers on the train.*

"Do you really think I could get a whole Bible into prison? It would be confiscated! But I do have the Gospel of Mark. That's part of the Bible," I said.

"Let's see it!" demanded one of the young men.

I opened my bag and pulled out the box with the little Gospel. Hands stretched out from all directions to touch it. "It's so tiny!" the prisoners marveled. Everyone wanted to see it.

"Can we read it?" asked the man in the black sweater.

"Yes, of course!" I handed it to him.

Suddenly the skinny little old man darted forward and grabbed for the little book. "Don't touch it!" he cried. "It's a holy book and our hands are sinful! They're stained with human blood! Have him read it to us!"

The man in the black sweater pulled free from his grasp. His gaze shifted from the little old man to the Gospel still in his hand and then to me.

"Don't be afraid," I urged. "This book was written for you as well as for me. It holds the path to salvation and a new life."

I stood, still holding my bag. Weariness overcame me. I didn't know how much longer I could stand. A young man turned to me. "You can have my bunk tonight." Then to the others he sneered, "Ha! Why are you attacking him like animals? The man's been in prison for years only for his faith in God and you harass him! Sit down here." He showed me his bunk.

"Where are you from?" he asked.

"Kiev."

"I'm from Kiev, too! I spent a month there robbing. That's where I was arrested the last time. What camp were you in?"

"Tabaga, a strict-regime camp about fifteen miles from Yakutsk," I answered.

Another prisoner confirmed my statement. "Oh, yes," he said, bobbing his head up and down, "I know that camp. What other camps are in Yakutia?"

I named at least three other camps in Yakutia where I had been a prisoner. Again other prisoners confirmed my words. Still holding the Gospel, the man in the black sweater sat down at the table. The rest of the men gathered around and he began reading aloud:

"The beginning of the gospel of Jesus Christ, the Son of God; As it is written in the prophets, Behold, I send my messenger before thy face, which shall prepare thy way before thee. . .

"Let us see it! Let me hold it! I want to at least touch it! I've never held a Gospel in my life!" interrupted excited voices.

Just then the metal door scraped open and an officer and two soldiers entered the cell. Even before the door was completely open, the man in the black sweater had managed to hand the little book to another prisoner who hopped up to his bunk in a flash. It happened so quickly that hardly anyone in the cell noticed.

"Why aren't you sleeping?" the officer asked. Then he looked straight at me. "How do you like your new cellmate? Is he one of you?"

Everyone was silent. The officer seemed quite disappointed. He studied my face to see if I'd been beaten. Now I understood why I'd been put in this cell. He had expected the murderers to attack me.

"Don't believe anything he says," the officer said, pointing his finger at me as he left.

After the officer was gone, the man in the black sweater retrieved the Gospel. I went over to a bunk, knelt, and poured out my thanksgiving to God.

"Look! He's praying!" whispered some of the prisoners in amazement. "Let him pray. It's his business," said others.

Complete peace filled my heart. Later I learned that the KGB had indeed instructed the prison administrators to put me in that specific cell. Some of the prisoners had been told lies about me in advance and were incited to attack me. I'm sure the KGB concealed the fact that I was a Christian. But with that little Gospel of Mark, God had, in an amazing way, upset the cunning schemes of His enemies. I felt completely secure, protected by God Himself.

A COPY OF THE GOSPEL OF MARK

YAKUTSK—COLDEST CITY ON EARTH

Yakutsk lies in the far-eastern part of Russia, about 450 kilometers south of the Arctic Circle. It holds the title of the coldest city on earth, with winter temperatures dropping below -50°C. It is the capital of the Sakha province. Yakutsk has a population of about 200,000, with a million people living in the rest of the region.

Most of Siberia is covered with up to 1,500 meters of permafrost. Buildings and houses in the city are built on stilts, about 2 meters above the surface. During the Siberian summer, temperatures can rise to 30° and more. Up to 3 meters of soil can thaw and the earth gets wet and muddy. The foundations of the houses must be built into the permafrost ground because the thawed layer is unstable and can move easily.

Yakutsk is six time zones away from the capital, Moscow. A plane trip takes about 6 hours. The other possibility is to go up the Lena River by boat. The road to Yakutia was built by former labor camp inmates. It is used mostly by trucks that bring supplies to remote villages.[1]

SIBERIAN LANDSCAPE

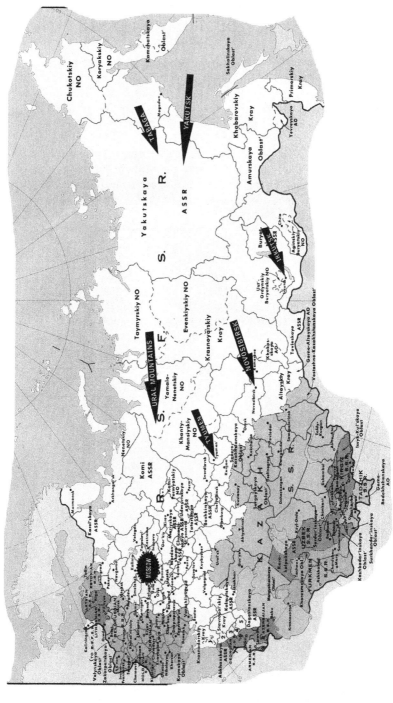

MAP OF THE U.S.S.R. | ARROWS POINT TO SOME OF THE PRISONS AND PRISON CAMPS GEORGI VINS WAS IN

16

A WEEK AMONG MURDERERS

When I awoke the next morning I didn't remember where I was. Then I opened my eyes and saw the other prisoners sitting around the table, listening intently as one of them read from the Gospel. Already the morning sun penetrated the double-barred window of the cell as a fresh breeze blew through a small open pane. I lay quietly, listening to the Word of God. Soon the closing verse of Mark 16 was read. I got up and walked to the table, and the man in the black sweater handed me the Gospel. Everyone was silent.

"It's a powerful book," he said simply.

The little old man turned to me. "I've killed five people," he said. "Can God forgive me?"

The man in the black sweater looked at me closely. "How can I find salvation? All night we were reading the Gospel and discussing this. There was no one to ask and we didn't want to wake you. I'm also a murderer, a murderer and a thief. That's what the Gospel said.

How can we get this salvation?"

"If you repent before God and trust in Jesus Christ, then you, too, will receive salvation," I told the man in the black sweater. "And God will help you turn from your wicked, criminal life."

The little old man's voice trembled with fear and excitement. "But I've killed five men. This isn't even the first time I've been caught. I was in prison before, you know. They wanted to execute me but changed my sentence to fifteen years' special strict regime. Do you think God can forgive even me?" he asked.

I looked at the puny man with the squeaky voice. How odd that such a feeble person could find strength to kill five people. "Yes, God can forgive you," I said. "Jesus Christ forgave the criminal on the cross next to Him. He took everyone's sins upon Himself, even the most horrible sins, and died on the Cross for all men because God loves us. Even though I never killed anyone or stole anything, I am a sinner, too, a sinner forgiven by Jesus Christ and saved." And I recited the familiar verse of John 3:16: "For God so loved the world, that he gave his only begotten Son, that whosoever believeth in him, should not perish but have everlasting life."

"Have any of you ever read the Bible before or heard a sermon about Jesus Christ?" I asked.

They shook their heads. Never before in their lives had any of these men read the Gospel or heard a sermon. Seeing this, I was again amazed that after reading it just one night, they understood the Gospel's main message—salvation! Usually prisoners are proud of their criminal exploits. They don't even use the words "kill" or "murder." They say, "Well, I got him wet" (meaning wet with blood), or "wasted him," or "squeezed him." And when they talk about it, their victim was invariably the guilty one who got what he deserved. But after reading the Gospel, these men understood that they were the guilty ones, they were the criminals, they were the sinners, having sinned not only against man but, more importantly, against God.

I spent a week in that cell. The men asked hundreds of questions. Every day we talked about God. I explained how Jesus died on the Cross—not for His wrongdoing but to pay the penalty—serve the sentence—for our sins, our crimes. If we believe that He died in our place, He offers us a new life, a fresh start, doing what pleases God. He gives us hope for the future and strength to make it through each day.

The men listened tirelessly. It was hard to believe that these same men had been so hostile toward me that first, tense night. I rejoiced at what God was doing in their hearts. But I knew that it was only the beginning. I can't say that all of them repented and became Christians right there, but I saw their desire to learn about God.

My "neighbor" from Kiev, whose name was Petro, stayed by my side for hours at a time. He had spent his whole life engaged in various criminal activities. Petro was fascinated by everything I had to say and asked many questions. He simply couldn't understand why the authorities were so cruel to Christians.

"You are a believer," he'd say. "Why do they put you in prison? You can help people!"

One day the cell door opened and a guard called out my name. "Gather your things and get ready to move," he said.

He left, giving me ten minutes to prepare for the journey. I looked at my cellmates. One of them hurried over to me and held out my tiny Gospel of Mark. "It was absolutely amazing that we could read it here in prison," he said. "Thank you."

Petro looked at me longingly as I hid the little book in my bag. "Oh, Georgi," he cried, "give us that Gospel! You already know the story. You've read it many times but we just started reading it. We've all got fifteen years to go through. And some of us," he glanced at the little old man, "will probably die in camp. We really need that holy book. Please leave it with us!"

What should I do? I wondered. *This little book is so precious to me! I've had it so many years in prisons and camps.* The Lord preserved it through many searches, even on the train when the soldiers found it and wanted me to rip it up. This little book actually saved my life in this cell. *I still have exile. Oh, I don't want to give it up!*

"Your God will give you many Gospels," added the man in the black sweater. "Where will we get another one? Leave it with us. It's the only truth I've found in my whole life."

I handed it back to the man in the black sweater.

"Get moving! Let's get out of here!" the guard shouted impatiently through the door.

I grabbed my bag. Someone quickly shook my hand as we parted. "Farewell, Georgi! Pray for us!"

The guard took me to the transit cell. I was so impressed by my week in the cell with the murderers that I nearly forgot about being exiled to Tyumen. With my own eyes, I saw how special God's Word became to those prisoners in such a short time. I'll never forget them. I left behind with them not only my tiny Gospel of Mark, but also part of my heart.

But other dangers lay ahead.

1976—DURING HIS FAMILY VISIT AT
YAKUTSK PRISON CAMP

17

THE TRANSIT CELL

The transit cell is a place of continual activity. Prisoners are constantly either being brought in or taken out, just like at a train station. The Novosibirsk prison has several transit cells, holding several hundred prisoners waiting to be sent in all directions. Some go east in Siberia, others west to the Urals or south to Kazakhstan. There were no bunks in my next cell. About one hundred men sat on the floor waiting to continue their journey.

Near the tiny window was a single wooden bench occupied by five men. After the guard locked the door behind me, I sat on the floor, my back against the cement wall. Some of the prisoners looked at me listlessly. I didn't recognize anyone, but I noticed that the five sitting on the bench were studying me.

No sooner had I slumped to the floor when one of the prisoners on the bench shouted, "Why are you hiding by the door?"

"I know his kind. They have money! Get over here!" snarled another.

I remained silent. *Oh, Lord*, I prayed, *what's going on now?*

Another testing! Lord Jesus, be with me! Then it became clear. Not succeeding in their plan with the murderers' cell, the KGB had apparently spread the word that I had money in order to incite some of the prisoners against me.

The cell suddenly became quiet. Two men on the bench got up and started making their way toward me.

"You have money? It's better to give it to us now!" they threatened.

I stood. "I have no money."

"Then why were you crouching by the door? You won't have time to call a guard! We'll strangle you!" shouted another.

About ten men on that side of the cell rose to their feet and began insulting and cursing me.

"Why are you swearing at me?" I asked loudly. "Who told you to do that? The prison officials? I'm a Christian. I've been in prison eight years already. But even here, the KGB won't leave me alone. What do you want from me?"

"Do you have money?" the man asked again, this time more calmly.

"I already told you that I'm a Christian. Money in prison just leads to fighting and murder. I don't have any money, and I don't want any," I replied evenly.

One of the men on the bench smiled at me. "Come sit here," he invited, moving over to make room for me.

I sat on the bench. Once again, the Lord had calmed the chaos. My soul quietly rejoiced in Him.

"So who are you? Where are you from? What do you know about the Bible? What kind of faith do you have? What is faith?" The questions showered upon me.

A hush settled over the cell as everyone waited for my answers. I began telling the men about God and new life in Jesus Christ. Twenty minutes later the door opened and several names were called, including mine. It was time to go.

Just before I left, one of the prisoners turned to me and whispered, "They wanted to kill you here! They were going to stuff a rag in your mouth and beat you. Men were talking about you before you even came. Someone told them you had lots of money sewn into your jacket. They didn't know you're a Christian. It's amazing how you handled them!"

But I knew that it was the Lord's power and His protection that had saved me.

"Well, do you have any money?" he asked hopefully.

"Of course not," I answered.

Another routine search and I was put on a train car heading west toward the Urals. *What lies ahead? Oh, Lord, only You know!*

The name of the Lord
is a strong tower: the
righteous runneth
into it, and is safe.
(Proverbs 18:10)

In the barracks where we lived, we three [prisoners] prayed openly by our plank beds. We talked just as openly about God with the people around us. The prisoners, and also the soldiers and officers of the guard, showed great interest, and asked us numerous questions: about the reason for our arrests, about our faith, about the Bible, about God. We tried to give thorough Christian answers to all these questions. Some of the prisoners stopped smoking and swearing, and even began to pray. All this greatly troubled not only the local camp authorities, but also Moscow.[1]

— *Prison Camp Diary
1967 during Georgi's first
imprisonment*

THE ACCUSATIONS BY THE SOVIET GOVERNMENT AGAINST GEORGI VINS

1. Violation of the law on religious cults which involves: Ban on all missionary activity, inviting young people into the church, Christian education of children. It is regarded as a criminal article in the USSR.

2. Falsification of Soviet reality through news and information about the persecution and imprisonments of believers.

3. Violations of rights of citizens, e.g., any sermon calling for conversion or, more precisely, any missionary activity. This is the strongest article, which also refers to damaging citizens' health. "Under the pretext of religion, violence is practiced on a person's body and the moral life is destroyed." In contrast to the other two which entail three years' imprisonment, violation of this article entails ten years: five years' labor camp and five years' exile.[1]

— LYDIA VINS IN DEFENDING HER SON TO THE COURT

18

THE EXILE'S NEW CLOTHES

From Novosibirsk I was taken to the prison in Tyumen. My cell was overcrowded, and many of us had to sleep on the cement floor. There was no relief from the stinging cigarette smoke hanging in thick clouds in the dank, heavy air. I longed to be in exile, even in the remotest part of Siberia where I would have a small room with my own bed, plenty of fresh air to breathe, and no guards. The fact that my prison term had actually ended weeks earlier and I should already have been in exile made it harder to bear.

After lunch on April 25, 1979, I was summoned for a meeting. I'd never been to Tyumen before and didn't know anyone here, so who would come to visit me? It was probably a mistake. But when the guard opened the door of the meeting room, I saw my wife Nadia! What was she doing here? How did she find out where I was? She smiled at me through the thick glass partition that separated us. A guard explained the rules of the meeting. We could not see each other except through the thick glass and could communicate only through telephone receivers. An officer listened to every word of our conversation through a third receiver.

"Nadia, how did you get here?" I asked. "Is everything all right at home? How are the children? Is Mama ill?"

She told me that for two months they hadn't received any letters from me. When my prison term ended in March, they sent a telegram to the camp in Tabaga. The camp director told them that I had been put on a transport several weeks earlier, but he didn't know where I had been taken. As time passed and there was still no word of my whereabouts, my family started to worry. After much prayer, they decided that Nadia would look for me in various Siberian prisons, starting with Tyumen. If I wasn't there, she would travel east to Novosibirsk, Krasnoyarsk, and Yakutsk until she found me.

Nadia said that she had arrived in Tyumen the day before. She was excited when officials told her that not only was I here, but we could have a meeting! We were amazed at how the Lord directed her to the exact city where I was.

Our meeting lasted two hours. I learned that my children were impatient to visit me in exile. I asked Nadia to stop in Moscow on the way back to Kiev and petition the authorities to send me to my place of exile as soon as possible because conditions at the Tyumen prison were unbearable.

Then our meeting ended and we parted. I was taken back to my prison cell and my wife began her journey back to Kiev.

The next day, guards informed me that I was being moved to Moscow. I was alarmed. What had happened? My place of exile was near Tyumen. The reply was customary: "You're a prisoner and not allowed to ask questions. Just get ready."

The raven took me to the airport where I boarded a passenger airplane. Seated between guards, I was flown to Moscow and taken to one of the prisons there.

This is certainly strange, I thought. *What's going on? Am I going to be tried again? Maybe some other Christian leaders were arrested and there will be a joint trial and I'll be sentenced again.* That was the only logical explanation I could think of for my transfer to Moscow. I couldn't sleep that night. I prayed a lot and again committed my life into the Lord's hands.

The next morning, Friday, April 27, a guard woke me early and told me to shower. The first thing in the morning? I was really surprised. Nothing like this ever happened before in my prison life.

He took me to a shower room and left me alone. After I was through, I waited for the guard to return my clothes. Prisoners' clothes are routinely fumigated against lice. Usually they are ready and waiting by the time you're finished with your shower. After about five minutes, I began to wonder why they were taking so long to return my clothes.

Suddenly an officer with the rank of captain appeared. "Why aren't you dressed?" he asked.

"I'm waiting for my clothes," I answered.

"What? Your clothes are right over there," he said, pointing to a nearby chair. On the chair lay a dark suit, a white shirt, a necktie, socks, and a pair of shoes. I hadn't paid any attention to them because they weren't mine.

"Get dressed," the officer ordered.

"Where is my uniform?" I asked.

"Just wear what is on the chair."

"First tell me what this is all about," I said. "These aren't my things. What's happening?"

"Prisoners aren't allowed to ask questions. The administration gives the orders. Get dressed," he repeated.

Hurriedly I dressed. For the first time in five years, I put on a new white shirt, a new suit, and a tie. The officer left and a barber came in carrying a white smock, a razor, and everything necessary for shaving. "Do you want a shave?" he asked.

"Just a trim," I said. Being on the transport and in transit prisons, I hadn't shaved for two months and decided to keep the beard. Still I wondered what was happening. For a prisoner to have his own personal barber was really something!

After a while, the captain returned. "Follow me!" he ordered, and led me down the corridor to an office. As I went in, he disappeared down the hall. Behind a desk sat a high-ranking official. He stood and handed me a document.

"Read this," he said.

It was a decree from the Presidium of the Supreme Soviet of the U.S.S.R. stating that I was being stripped of my Soviet citizenship and would be exiled to the United States of America.

Silence filled the room. The official looked at me. "Do you understand that you're being expelled from the territory of the Soviet Union and that you are no longer a citizen of the U.S.S.R.?" he asked.

"I understand," I said, "but I don't agree to this. Can a person really be deprived of his citizenship and exiled from his homeland because of religious activities?"

The official cut me off, saying that the decision had been made by the highest authority in the country and the matter was now closed. Then he informed me that in two hours I would no longer be on Soviet soil.

"You are the most unfortunate person in the world," he added condescendingly. "You are a man with no citizenship, no homeland, no roots. You're being sent to America. Maybe for a week or two you'll cause quite a sensation there, but soon everyone will forget about you. Nobody there needs you."

The official went on to say that my family could follow me to America if they so desired.

"I need to talk with my family and discuss this with them, even if it's only by telephone," I said.

"No. It's forbidden."

Armed guards came and escorted me to a waiting car. I sat in the back seat between two guards. We were in one of a whole line of cars, all which quickly accelerated and sped off for Sheremetyevo Airport.

The guards whisked me and four other prisoners onto an Aeroflot jet. A Soviet medical doctor was assigned to travel with us, and twenty plainclothes KGB agents guarded us on that flight to New York. After we were seated, civilian passengers boarded the plane.

We prisoners were not allowed to speak to anyone during that ten-hour flight. So many thoughts crowded my weary mind as I stared out the window. *Lord, why are You taking me to this foreign country? I don't know anyone in America. I don't speak English. What will it be like? When will I see my family again?*

I also thought about the parting words of the Soviet official, who said I no longer had a homeland. But who can deprive me of my heavenly citizenship? Who can separate me from God? No one! The Lord will never abandon me no matter where I am. My God was powerful enough to protect me and care for me at the worst moments of my prison life, and He would continue to care for me even in the unknown land of America.

> Who shall separate us from the love of Christ? shall tribulation, or distress, or persecution, or famine, or nakedness, or peril, or sword? (Romans 8:35)

After the plane landed at Kennedy Airport in New York, we five prisoners and our guards remained seated while the other passengers got off the plane. Then the plane taxied to an isolated runway and we were ordered to leave the aircraft. The guards didn't follow us. Although we didn't know it at the time, at the same moment two Soviet spies captured by the Americans were boarding through a different door. Later we learned that an agreement had been negotiated between President Jimmy Carter and Premier Leonid Brezhnev to exchange five prisoners for the two spies.

Several officials from the U.S. State Department met us as soon as our feet touched American soil and congratulated us on our freedom. Then we were taken by car to a Hilton Hotel. Each of us was given a private room on the 36th floor. When I found a Bible on my nightstand, I thought that probably the Americans had put one in my room because they knew I was a Christian. Unfortunately, it was in English. I mentioned this to a State Department official and later that night, an anonymous New Yorker brought me a Russian Bible. After five years, I finally had my own Bible!

The next morning, newspaper, radio, and television correspondents arrived to interview us. Later that day at a large press conference, each of us former prisoners made a statement through an interpreter. When my turn came, I lifted my Russian Bible high and said, "I'm the happiest person in the world. I now have my own Bible and no one will take it away from me!"

GEORGI—IN HIS FIRST FEW DAYS IN THE U.S.

I could tell by their expressions that the journalists didn't understand what was so special about having a Bible. They didn't know what it meant for a Christian to go many years without God's Word.

President Carter saw that news program and wanted to meet me, so later that day I flew to Washington, D.C., accompanied by representatives of the State Department and an interpreter.

On Sunday morning, I met President Carter at the First Baptist Church. We had a twenty-minute conversation, during which I presented the situation of the persecuted believers in my homeland and told him about those who remained in prisons, labor camps, and psychiatric hospitals for their faith.

President Carter invited me to his Sunday school class. I sat between Mrs. Carter and an interpreter. About one hundred people listened as the President opened God's Word and taught a lesson from the book of Esther. He also spoke about my release. "We've prayed many years for Georgi Vins, our brother in Christ," he said. "God has answered our prayers. It was neither I nor the Congress nor the American negotiators who freed him. God Himself did it and He deserves all the credit."

I marveled at the United States president holding a Bible in his hands, treating it with respect and teaching from it. How different from the leaders in my own country who were confiscating and burning Bibles and putting Christians in prison for preaching from that book! I will never forget that day.

During the Sunday school hour, I also thought about the little Gospel of Mark left in that prison cell in Novosibirsk. As I held my Bible and prayed silently for those murderers, I suddenly recalled the parting words of the man in the black sweater: "Give us this Gospel. Your God will give you many Bibles and Gospels . . ."

Today I do have many Bibles, many Gospels, but my little Gospel of Mark remained behind bars in Siberia. What became of my Gospel in bonds? What became of those men in the murderers' cell? I'm convinced that the Lord Himself will take care of them. Surely God will send other Christian men who will water the seed that was sown in their souls. But I won't learn about that until I get to heaven.

> Wherefore, though I might be much bold in Christ to enjoin thee that which is convenient, yet for love's sake I rather beseech thee . . . and now also a prisoner of Jesus Christ. . . . that in thy stead he might have ministered unto me in the bonds of the gospel. (Philemon 1: 8-9, 13)

THE FIRST MORNING IN US—HIS EYES PORTRAY THE GRIEF FROM PARTING WITH HIS NATIVE LAND BUT ALSO QUIETLY TRUSTING THE LORD FOR THE UNKNOWN FUTURE

FIRST WEEK OF FREEDOM

19

NEW FRIENDS

Lord, out of all the prisoners, why did you choose me for freedom? And what about my family? Do they know what has happened? What awaits me in America? Stripped of my soviet citizenship, now I'm a man without a country. Yet I know my true citizenship is in heaven. Those were the questions I pondered as the plane left the runway at Sheremetyevo Airport. I sought to fix my mind on God, praying through the long flight from Moscow to New York.

Although I was now free, many of my Christian brothers and sisters remained behind bars. Right then, on that very first day, the Lord laid on my heart a firm resolve to always stand with the persecuted church. This would be my ministry, my life in the free world.

The next day the Lord gave me the opportunity to greet my family and friends on a Voice of America radio broadcast:

"I wish to greet my fellow Christians of the Soviet Union with these verses from God's Word: 'I thank my God through Jesus Christ for you all, that your faith is spoken of throughout the whole world. For God is my witness, whom I serve with my spirit in the Gospel of his Son, that without ceasing I make mention of you always in my prayers; making request, if by any means now at length I might have a prosperous journey by the will of God to come unto you' (Romans 1:8-10).

"Dear brothers and sisters, your faith is spoken of throughout the whole world! I especially wish to greet all our co-workers in God's ministry. I wish to greet those who are printing Bibles, the workers of the Christian Publishing House. Special greetings to the Council of Prisoners' Relatives, who unceasingly raise prayers and petitions on behalf of all who are persecuted for the Word of God. To all my brothers and sisters of the persecuted church, to all who love the Lord, and especially to those who are ambassadors in bonds, I extend my most heartfelt greetings.

"Though I am now in a strange new place, my heart and thoughts remain closely bound to my beloved people, the Russians, Ukrainians, and all the peoples of the Soviet Union. I greet you with the love of our Lord Jesus Christ!"

Two months later the persecuted Baptist churches in the Soviet Union commissioned me to be their representative in the West. In 1980, an office was opened in Elkhart, Indiana, to represent, defend, and aid them. Our stated goals included: representing the persecuted church and Council of Evangelical Baptist Churches before the worldwide family of Christians; distributing information concerning the life and ministry of Christians in the U.S.S.R.; organizing aid for Christians in the U.S.S.R. by providing Bibles, assisting the Christian Publishing House, and supporting the families of Christian prisoners; and preaching the Gospel on radio broadcasts to the Soviet Union.

During the years of our ministry, we have discovered that persecuted Christians have thousands of friends in the United States, Canada, and around the world. I wish to thank each of you who have been standing with us in support of those who suffer for the Lord's sake. Let us never forget their message to Christians living in the free world: "Live in such a way that your prayers for us will be heard!"

The Lord heard the weeping of His suffering people and the prayers of Christians around the world. By December 1988, all Evangelical Baptist prisoners were released. In addition, the Lord opened wide the door to send Bibles to the Soviet Union. Since then, many people have heard of Jesus Christ for the first time and have come to know him as Savior. To God be the glory!

As all the other prisoners and exiles returned home, hope stirred again in my heart. The apostle Paul's prayer became my own:

> For God is my witness, whom I serve with my spirit in the gospel of his Son, that without ceasing I make mention of you always in my prayers; Making request, if by any means now at length I might have a prosperous journey by the will of God to come unto you. (Romans 1:8-10)

Would I ever go home again?

AFTER HIS RELEASE, WHENEVER GEORGI SPOKE TO GROUPS,
HE WOULD HOLD UP PICTURES OF BELIEVERS WHO WERE
STILL BEING PERSECUTED BECAUSE OF COMMUNISM

MEETING WITH THEN PRESIDENT REAGAN AT THE WHITE HOUSE

GEORGI'S REUNION DAY WITH HIS FAMILY IN THE USA—PICTURED
HERE WITH HIS MOTHER, LYDIA, AND HIS SON, ALEX

1981—INDIANA—FROM LEFT: NADIA, JANE, LYDIA, LISA, GEORGI, ALEX, AND NATASHA

1982—INDIANA—STANDING FROM LEFT: ALEX, JANE, PETER, LISA, GEORGI; SITTING FROM LEFT: NATASHA, LYDIA, NADIA

GEORGI CONTINUED SPEAKING OUT AROUND THE WORLD
ON BEHALF OF PERSECUTED BROTHERS AND SISTERS

A COMMUNION AND WORSHIP SERVICE IN THE PERSECUTED CHURCH
IN 1984 IN KIEV, UKRAINE

20

HOME AGAIN!

November 15, 1990, O'Hare International Airport in Chicago. Nadia and I were waiting to board a Sabena Airlines' jet to begin our journey back to the USSR. For eleven years, it had seemed that such a moment would never be more than a dream. But on August 15, 1990, Soviet president Mikhail Gorbachev had issued a decree rescinding the edict of April 24, 1979, by which I had been stripped of my Soviet citizenship and exiled to America. Since then, how I'd longed to be back to my homeland and see my friends and relatives again! Now we really were on our way back.

From Chicago we flew to Brussels, where we transferred to Aeroflot. The TU-134 was only half full, the passengers were mostly Soviet tourists returning home and Belgian businessmen. Three hours after departing Brussels, our plane began its descent into Kiev, the capital of Ukraine. I looked impatiently through the window at the forest, the buildings, and the streets of Borispol, a suburb of Kiev. My heart leaped as the wheels touched the runway. Then we were taxiing to the gate. As the stairway was attached, everyone prepared to get off. Nadia and I were ready, too.

Finally, we were on native soil, walking to the airport terminal where we would wait to go through customs. Nadia was getting nervous. "We don't know what's waiting for you here. What if they don't let you through?" she whispered. "We shouldn't have come alone. There's no one to keep an eye on us, to see if we make it safely through. What if they're laying a trap for you?" Then she spotted a Belgian businessman who had sat near us on the plane.

"Could you please do us a favor?" she asked in English. "Would you just watch to see how we make it through customs? My husband was exiled from the country for religious activity eleven years ago, and now we're back for our first visit. I'm worried that we might have some complications."

The Belgian agreed. "Sure, I'll watch. But I don't think you'll have any problems. I'm well acquainted with this country. Things have really changed."

He passed through customs ahead of us, then stood to the side to see how things went for us. Praise the Lord, there were no problems. The Belgian waved and joined his waiting friends.

Nadia's brother met us at the airport. The next day was Sunday, and we planned to attend the worship service at our home church. How well I remembered my last service in Kiev! It was August 1970. We'd gathered in the forest near Kiev. I was preaching when about twenty policemen and KGB seemed to come out of nowhere and broke up the service. I never preached in Kiev again, because I went underground until my arrest and ten-year sentence. Now, twenty years later, the worship services were held in a simple wooden building in the backyard of Pastor Yakov Ivaschenko's home on the outskirts of Kiev.

Nadia and I hadn't had a chance to tell anyone that we were coming. We arrived just ten minutes before the service began. As my wife helped my elderly aunt out of the car, I quietly slipped inside, hung up my coat, and sat down on a wooden bench. At first, I didn't recognize anyone, since most of those present had young, unfamiliar faces and many children. I studied the faces and finally picked out a few familiar ones, older than I remembered, now with gray hair. I noticed many people studying me, too, as if they knew me from somewhere, but couldn't quite place my face. Just then, Nadia, her brother, and my aunt entered the building. Suddenly people knew who we were and ran to greet us. Such a joyful, excited welcome!

The service started, I was asked to preach. Tears stung my eyes as I made my way to the pulpit. I spoke on Matthew 5:10-12:

> Blessed are they which are persecuted for righteousness' sake: for theirs is the kingdom of heaven. Blessed are ye, when men shall revile you, and persecute you, and shall say all manner of evil against you falsely, for my sake.

This topic seemed appropriate because of what the Kiev church had suffered for so long. Only in the past two years had they been able to conduct worship services without being interrupted by the KGB and militia.

Two other ministers, both in their thirties, also preached. I knew them when they were children, and here they were, serving the Lord! Although twenty years had passed, the spirit of the services remained the same. It was wonderful to hear sermons and to sing hymns about Christ in my native language. After the service came the joy of personal greetings, introductions, and endless questions.

In the evening, Nadia and I went to church in Belaya Tserkov, about sixty miles from Kiev. The unregistered Baptist congregation there was greatly persecuted in the past and was often fined for holding worship services. Many of its preachers were imprisoned for their ministries. For many years, the congregation met in people's homes, but about two years earlier, a tall, spacious building made of boards and plywood was built for worship services.

After the meeting, Nadia and I had joyful reunions with believers whom we had not seen for many years, and the teenagers asked me to speak to their large youth group. (About 80 percent of that congregation is young people 15-30 years of age!)

Monday evening we had a family reunion. I hadn't seen some of my cousins for more than twenty years! I was glad to meet their spouses, children, and grandchildren. I had a wonderful opportunity to tell them about the Lord and to give them New Testaments.

On Tuesday I was taken to the Baptist church in Cherkassy, 120 miles from Kiev. Nadia stayed in Kiev to visit more with relatives. The church in Cherkassy is lively and friendly. Their pastor, Nikolai Shepel, is a former prisoner. The service there lasted over three hours. I didn't get back to Kiev until 4:00 a.m.

NOVEMBER 1990—FIRST TIME PREACHING AGAIN IN KIEV AFTER 8 YEARS OF IMPRISONMENT AND 11 YEARS IN THE UNITED STATES

On Thursday, Nadia and I visited the Baptist church in Vinnitsa, 180 miles from Kiev. The meeting was held in the home of the pastor, Nikolai Mashnitsky, who had been imprisoned twice. His son Peter, a young preacher, had also been in prison for his faith. In the past the authorities had persecuted this church harshly, especially trying to force the Mashnitsky family to stop holding services in their home. The police and the KGB broke up the services, arrested people, fined Mrs. Mashnitsky while her husband was in prison, and even tried to tear down the house. All of this went on for almost twenty years, right up until 1989. But, with the Lord's help, the church survived these trials and services continued to be held in the Mashnitsky home.

On Friday evening, many believers gathered at Kiev train station to see my wife and me off to Kharkov. We prayed and sang. I preached a short sermon, challenging the believers to evangelize not only their own city, but also the eastern regions of the country, the Urals, Siberia, and the Far East.

No one bothered us at the station or tried to interfere. How unlike a memorable summer day in 1963! We'd gathered in the forest near Kiev for our worship service, when the KGB and police suddenly burst in on us and began beating the believers. Then they forced us onto a commuter train back to Kiev. At this very same station, believers were once again beaten, and nineteen of us were put in prison. That was my first short imprisonment, only fifteen days. And so it was with those fifteen days in the Kiev prison in 1963 that I began my years of prison journeys.

And now freedom. I looked around at the dear faces of my Kiev friends. *When will we meet again? Only God knows.* The train jerked into motion. Last words of good-bye. *God be with you, dear friends. May He preserve you in His love!*

The next morning we arrived in Kharkov for another joyful reunion with friends at the train station there. In the past, during persecution, I had been in Kharkov dozens of times, preaching in the services, meeting with ministers, and sharing the joys and sorrows on the narrow and thorny path of Christians.

Nadia and I attended several meetings in churches in Kharkov. The services were filled to overflowing and lasted three to four hours. Believers came from as far away as the Urals, the Caucasus, and Moldavia. Many couldn't fit into the building, so they stood outside and listened by way of the loudspeakers. One evening was set aside for fellowship with local pastors. About fifty ministers gathered, many of whom had been imprisoned for their faith. All of them had many questions about the Lord's work in the West, especially America.

After one of the services, a man walked up to me and said, "My name is Anatoly. Do you remember me? In 1974, you and I were cell mates in Kiev. If memory serves me right, it was cell 84. There I first heard about Christ as my personal Savior through your testimony. Now I am a Christian!"

I was surrounded by people who wanted to talk, so Anatoly and I had only a few minutes together. He handed me a letter describing how he finally came to the Lord. I found out that after our talks about God in the Kiev prison, the Lord had kept after Anatoly.

In 1976, Anatoly was imprisoned again in the city of Chernigov, where he met Stepan Makhovik, who had been sentenced for preaching the Gospel. Makhovik told Anatoly about the Lord and the way of salvation. Anatoly's heart became inclined to accept the Word of God, and he even began to pray, but the pull of the criminal life was stronger than his aspirations to come to God, and Anatoly once more plunged into sin.

Years passed: prison, labor camp, release, then another crime and again back to prison. But the Lord did not stop knocking at Anatoly's heart. In 1985, he again ended up in a labor camp for his fifth term. It was there that he came across Viktor Mosha, a pastor from Kharkov sentenced for preaching the Gospel. Concerning this, Anatoly wrote in his note: "The Lord continuously put His faithful children in my path. In that camp with Viktor, I sincerely repented.

VIKTOR MOSHA

I have been out of the camps for three years now."

Here in America and in other free countries Christians have special ministries to reach prisoners. Pastors and evangelists can freely visit jails to talk with inmates, give out Gospels and tracts, and preach, urging souls to repentance and faith in Christ. But for decades in the Soviet Union, the Lord sent His faithful servants to the prisons and labor camps as prisoners themselves, where they, enduring all the hardships of prison and camp life, witnessed of God's love to thousands of criminals and even the officers and soldiers guarding them.

We know that the bonds of our brothers and sisters in the faith were not in vain. The Bible says, "They that sow in tears shall reap in joy. He that goeth forth and weepeth, bearing precious seed, shall doubtless come again with rejoicing, bringing his sheaves with him" (Psalm 126:5-6).

Today Anatoly lives near Kharkov with his Christian wife and children. In closing his note, he wrote, "I love Christian poetry, and your poems are especially dear to me and my family. Not only because I was personally acquainted with you, but because my family and I want to learn faithfulness to Jesus Christ!"

Praise God for this man who loves the Lord and desires to remain faithful to Him! Please pray for others who heard the Gospel in prison.

During one of the services in Kharkov, a former prosecutor from Kivertsy told the following story of how she came to faith in Christ two years earlier: "I am one of those who persecuted the church. I grew up in a non-Christian family. After graduating from a political institute, I worked in the prosecutor's office and carried out atheistic work based on the assignment to fight religion and believers, according to Stalin's anti-religious laws of 1929. I didn't like Christians, and I gave them contemptuous nicknames.

"One day in 1983 the city prosecutor of Kivertsy called me aside and said, 'You are to conduct a house search at the home of Ivan Kravchuk, a Baptist minister.' I agreed but asked, 'Where is Kravchuk now?' The prosecutor answered, 'In prison.' And so I led a group in conducting a house search. When we got there the house was locked, but Mrs. Kravchuk was outside. She wasn't feeling well. She already had five little children to care for and was expecting the sixth in about a week. I said to her, 'Open the door. If you don't, we'll break it down. We are here to search your house.' She opened without complaining.

"When I entered the house, I don't know why, but for some reason I couldn't conduct the search with zeal. We took a Bible and other Christian books. Soon after that, Kravchuk was sentenced to two and one-half years in labor camp. After the trial, I

> "What harm did he do to anybody, to people or society? Can it be it was all just for his faith in God? Now we've robbed six little children of their father."

thought about it a lot. *Why did we put him on trial, anyway? What harm did he do to anybody, to people or society? Can it be it was all just for his faith in God? Now we've robbed six little children of their father.*

"There was no peace for my soul. My conscience judged me. In all my years of working as a prosecutor, not once had we ever accused a Christian of hooliganism, drunkenness, robbery, or even a traffic violation. I pondered this. Now I know that the Lord was beginning His work in my heart. Only now do I understand that God had long ago started leading me through these contacts with believers. He took me through illness, and through family troubles. My husband was a drunk. In 1979 I divorced him.

"Kravchuk was sentenced on October 6, 1983. I remember it

well. The accuser at the trial was the prosecutor Sergei Gavriliuk. I remember after the trial that he was upset that Kravchuk had gotten only two and one-half years. Gavriliuk said, 'If it was up to me, I would have given him ten years.'

"The next day in town, I saw the head of the local KGB. He called me over, and I noticed he looked frightened. He said, 'Did you hear that Gavriliuk died last night?' He was so scared that I got scared, too. We both decided that this was supernatural. We knew that Gavriliuk hated Christians and always treated them cruelly. He had wanted to sentence Kravchuk to ten years.

"After Kravchuk's trial, I decided to look for a new job. I felt that I couldn't take part in any more trials against Christians. I couldn't search their homes or confiscate Bibles and New Testaments.

"After Kravchuk finished his term, he came to see me, and spoke kindly with me while I still worked at the prosecutor's office. I thought to myself, *Anyone else in his place would have cursed me. But believers don't remember evil. Kravchuk came to see me as though nothing ever happened, and he wants to talk with me about God and faith.* Today, I understand that perhaps the tears of his wife and himself, and the prayers of my mother who had become a Christian in 1979, fell on good soil and grew in my heart because soon after that, not only I but my whole family began turning to God: my son, my husband, and daughter. My husband and I eventually remarried.

"When we started going to church, Eugene Pushkov was visiting Kovel to preach. We all went to hear him. The choir sang a beautiful song about heaven. When he gave an invitation for repentance, I couldn't sit still. My daughter and I were sitting together. Some kind of power drew and pushed me. Go forward today, now or never. My daughter and I were both crying. A lady sitting next to me whispered, 'If God's Spirit is speaking to you, don't resist. Go forward.' But another voice in my heart said, *Not today. This isn't your church. This isn't your pastor. Your mother's not here. And you didn't agree to this with your husband.*

"But the first voice won, and my daughter and I went to the front of the church and stood by the preacher. I had never prayed before in my life, and I didn't know what to say. I just said, 'God, forgive me for everything that I have done displeasing to You. I want to serve You. My husband is here, and if it's pleasing to You that he come to You, I would really like that.' Just then, my husband came forward. I was filled with joy—I can't express it, each person has to feel it for himself. I still experience that joy! It's something I never knew in life before. I had only known 'joy' that comes from power, and I thought that that's all that happiness meant. Once a brother in Christ told me, 'We have a greater power—to be called the children of God.'

"When I think about the lives of people who still don't know God, I feel so sorry for them that I cry. My father isn't saved, and none of my five brothers and sisters are saved. I always say to them, 'Look around, see how people are dying. Think about death and eternity.'

"Of course, my friends and acquaintances were all shocked that I'd repented. Everybody heard about it the next day, and for some reason, I was a little embarrassed. I had been the deputy prosecutor, and the local newspapers had always written about me in a positive light. Now everyone was talking. All my old friends from the police station and the prosecutor's office and the court asked me, 'Is it true that you became a Christian? Are you crazy?' A year earlier, if I'd heard the same thing about someone else, I, too, would have thought something had gone wrong with his head.

"As I waited for my baptism, I asked Pastor Kravchuk, 'Do you think I could be baptized in a different church in another city?' He said, 'Don't worry about it, when it's time for your baptism, we'll talk it over. Do you remember what Jesus said, that whoever is ashamed of Me before people, I will be ashamed of him before our Father in Heaven?'

"Nineteen people were in our group to be baptized. My husband and I were the oldest. The rest were all young people. A week before the baptism, I invited everyone I knew to come, and I wasn't embarrassed. I prayed for good weather, but I also wanted just a little rain. People said, 'How can you ask for both good weather and rain?'

"The day of our baptism, the weather was cool. When we got

to the lake, a lot of people were already there, as many as at a May Day celebration. Traffic was stopped. At first, people thought there must be a big funeral procession since there was a brass band. But you could tell from the music that it wasn't a funeral. More people joined the crowd until the small lake was completely surrounded. Everyone was very interested in what they were about to see. They'd heard that a prosecutor was going to be 'bathed'!

"As I changed into my white robes for the baptism, it got warmer outside. When the ministers went into the water and began praying with their hands raised, a cloud scuttled in front of the sun and it rained for a minute and then stopped. At that moment, I was convinced that God had heard even this little prayer.

"Many ministers from various cities were there. Policemen and people from the regional Party office also came, but nobody interfered. Just as I went into the water, an unbeliever shouted out, 'Drown her! Drown her!' Apart from that, it was a peaceful service. When I saw journalists there taking notes, I expected them to defame me in the newspapers. But a week later, a paper came out with an article titled, 'At the Pure Fountains.' I was amazed at such a positive report about our baptism. If this had happened just a few years ago, I would have ended up in prison. If I had openly spoken out as a believer once or twice, I would have been fined; the third time, arrested.

"Now I'd like to say that I'm satisfied with my life. As my daughter and I talk about God, I smile. I realize that these are hard times in our country. Everybody's worried about daily problems and nobody feels like singing. But at our house, we sing, we pray, and we rejoice. The only thing I regret is that I lived so many years without God. I thank the Lord that He put up with me so long. Now I'm asking Him to save my brothers and sisters. I pray that they will choose to serve Him. I stood before my church family in Kivertsy and asked them and God to forgive me for taking part in the persecution and for bringing suffering upon the church. Now I also want to ask forgiveness from Georgi Vins, and I want to ask for God's blessing on the work of all of our ministers, that He will give them wisdom and power to preach His Word and that thousands and even millions of people in our country might come to God."

From Kharkov, Nadia and I were to fly to Leningrad. About 200 believers accompanied us to the Kharkov airport along with their brass band. The sky was cloudy, and it rained off and on, but everyone had brought along an umbrella. In the square in front of the Kharkov airport, we prayed, sang, preached, and handed out Gospels and tracts. There was plenty of time as our flight was delayed two hours. When we started handing out the literature, one woman shouted, "I want Jesus! Give me Jesus!" It was the first time in her life she had heard about Jesus Christ. She was thrilled when we gave her a New Testament. Several policemen came, stood and listened, then moved off. The band played Christian hymns, which kept drawing new people to the crowd. Finally, our flight was announced and we said goodbye to our friends.

FYODOR MAKHOVITSKY

Two hours later, Nadia and I were in Leningrad where about twenty believers greeted us at the airport. Among them were former prisoners Fyodor Makhovitsky, Mikhail Azarov, Vasily Gritsenko, Vasily Ryzhuk, and Dmitri Minyakov. Pastor Makhovitsky and I had served our prison sentence together in the northern Urals in 1967.[1] Right there we gave thanks to the Lord for this amazing meeting after so many years of separation. How precious and joyful it was to be together again!

On Friday evening, a worship service was held at the Leningrad church. I preached and told about our ministry in America. The next day, early in the morning, Nadia and I flew to America. *Farewell, dear friends, farewell, Russia! Or, perhaps it's better to say, until we meet again. May it be soon!*

21

A YEAR LATER—1991

'**ve now been back to my homeland four times: to Moscow, Leningrad, Ukraine, Byelorussia, and to Siberia and the Far East. I visited many churches and many believers and saw many old friends. The strongest impression for me and for them was the miracle that we could even see each other again.**

Christians have noticed that all over the country people want to learn about God. So believers everywhere are taking opportunities to witness out on the streets, in prisons, hospitals, and even at labor camps. They're also visiting places where there never used to be any believers. They hold meetings and Bible studies in schools and universities, and they operate portable libraries with Christian books. For example, they set up a book table on a sidewalk, or even in a subway. Anybody who wants to take out a book shows his passport, and a Christian library worker records on a card the person's name and address. All over, from Ukraine to Siberia, such libraries are open once or twice a week for several hours.

The biggest portable library I saw was in downtown Novosibirsk, in an underground walkway that also serves as a subway entrance. It's a great spot because people constantly pass by. Pastors and lay people operate the "library"—several hundred books laid out on a big table. In the course of a year, about three thousand people have become regular readers, checking out one book at a time. I wondered whether people ever check out a book and "forget" to return it. The pastor said it happens, but rarely. Some of the readers begin to visit worship services at the church and many come to the Lord. At a service I preached in Novosibirsk two such readers got saved.

Today unbelievers have a great interest in the Bible. When I was in Novosibirsk with several preachers from America, a crowd formed quickly when we began preaching on the street. Then we started passing out New Testaments, and people urgently asked for them. Some wanted to give us money in exchange. I also had Gospels of John and said, "Here. Have a Gospel, please." My American friends did the same, even though they couldn't speak Russian, they could only say the word "Boag"—God. That day I gave out about two hundred books to people from various walks of life, both intelligentsia and simple folk. Only about five refused, saying, "No, I don't need God." All the rest eagerly accepted them.

Later that day our group left the library in the underground walkway and went up to ground level. We started to sing in English, then I preached in Russian, and the others preached in English with an interpreter. Many people stopped to listen and asked lots of questions afterward. Our general impression was that people were spiritually starved.

I talked about God with people on the streets, on buses and trains; and was amazed to see how open they were to talking about God. I can recall only one woman said, "God never did anything to help me. I don't want to hear about Him!" And a man once said, "I'm an atheist, and I'm staying an atheist." But there were very few such people.

I also had an opportunity to speak at a medical school in Kiev. About six hundred students and some professors gathered. For about two hours, we preached the Gospel then fielded questions. Pastor Ivan Antonov also participated. As a young man he had been trained in medicine, but was later imprisoned a total of twenty years for his faith, forfeiting his career as a doctor. Now he was able to speak about his faith in God to a group of medical professionals. We were amazed that the professors themselves had organized this meeting.

Such are the great changes that have happened in my homeland.

It was interesting to talk with the professors at the medical college. One was a woman who had recently put her trust in Christ but hadn't yet been baptized. She said her life had changed when she trusted Christ, and that even her relationship with her husband had improved. Her two children who are students in the medical college also believe in God.

Once I found myself sharing a train compartment with an officer. He asked who I was and what I was doing. I explained that I now live in America, that I had been exiled from the country. He said, "Forgive us, please. That was our people who did that. But now we think differently. We know that young people need religious morality." The next morning when it was time for breakfast, he offered me some food he had brought along for the journey and I presented him with a New Testament and my book of poems. "But I don't have anything to give you in return," he said, searching his pockets for a gift. He gave me his pen. We had a good talk. He told me, "I believe that God exists. I always felt there was some kind of higher power. I'm glad our country now has freedom of religion."

I was happy to meet such people. In the past, my own relatives didn't want to hear about God, but now they are willing to listen. One of my cousins said, "Nothing is left to me in life except Christ." He's a scholar in physics who had married later in his life, at the age of 42. His wife died of a heart attack some years ago and his two children are away from home at college. He feels very lonely. Two years ago I sent him a Bible, and now it's on his end table. He says, "Science gave me nothing, my health is gone, my wife is dead, and all I've got left is Jesus Christ."

For seventy years, the Soviet authorities kept saying that there is no God, that the soul doesn't exist, and that the Bible is a collection of myths. Now they see a catastrophe occurring, not just moral, but also economic and ecological. One example is Chernobyl—but there wasn't just one Chernobyl, there were several similar events in the Urals, in Kazakhstan. People just didn't know. Today people are living in a time of upheaval. They see that they were deceived. For decades they had been told, "Soon we'll have communism. Just work for it a little harder, work for it a little longer! It's right on the horizon."

But then people realized that no matter what they did, the ideal society wouldn't arrive. Communism was always like a bright dream on the horizon that they could never reach. Now people realize it was always a fantasy, an illusion, so they are unhappy and disappointed, searching for something meaningful to believe in. Now they perceive the Bible, the Gospel, as something new and valuable. But if this truth touches only a person's brain and not his heart, it is of no benefit.

I have been asked whether I think people will still be open to the Gospel if economic plans for reform go well. It's too early to judge about Russia, but I know the example of West Germany. After World War II, German cities were in ruins. When the country had great economic problems and a lack of food, the Germans were inclined toward the Bible and were open to God. But when Germany became economically strong again, few Germans were interested in hearing about God. I think it might be the same way in Russia. At the moment, people are seeking spiritual values, but this hunger for God's truth might not last long.

22

NINETY-SIX DOLLARS

While visiting Kiev in the summer of 1992, I decided to ask the public prosecutor of Kiev to review my court case and consider the possibility of a judicial change and rehabilitation.

My wife asked me, "Why do you want to do this? What do you need rehabilitation for? Do you want financial compensation for the eight years you spent in prison?"

"No," I answered her, "financial compensation isn't the question. Justice should prevail. I need an official document from the Kiev City Court that I am not a criminal and that the Bible is not a criminal book."

In the center of Kiev, on Kreschatik Street stands a tall building of the former city council. Now many various institutions are situated there, including the City Public Prosecutor. I entered and saw a policeman standing guard. I pulled out my American passport, approached the policeman, and said, "I'm from America. I'm here on important business to see the Kiev City Public Prosecutor." The policeman politely replied, "Go to room 104 on the first floor."

When I walked up to the door of that room, I read a notice that visitors were seen from two until five o'clock in the afternoon, but it was still morning. What should I do? Wait there for four hours? I didn't have a car, and to get around the city you take the subway, streetcar, bus, trolley, or most often, walk.

Sometimes it takes up to two hours to get from one end of the city to the other. So, I decided to knock on the door and try to make an appointment. Having knocked, I opened the door a little, and saw a woman sitting behind a desk in a large office.

"Excuse me," I said to her, "I've come from America, and I need some information."

"Come in!" The tall woman stood and walked over to shake hands. She invited me to take a seat, and asked, "What brings you here?"

I introduced myself. "I'm a former Soviet citizen, now I live in the United States of America. In 1974 I was arrested, held for ten months in the Kiev Lukyanovsky prison, then in January of 1975 was tried and sentenced by the Kiev City Court to ten years for preaching the Gospel. After the trial, I was taken to a strict-regime labor camp in the north near Yakutsk. In April of 1979, I was put on an airplane and taken under guard from Siberia to a prison in Moscow, where I was informed that by an edict of the Supreme Soviet of the USSR I had been deprived of my Soviet citizenship and I was to be immediately exiled from the USSR forever. Since that time, I have lived in America. However, in August of 1990, Mikhail Gorbachev, the President of the USSR, changed the edict of 1979, and returned my Soviet citizenship."

The woman listened to me with great interest.

"I came here to find out," I continued, "to whom I should appeal to review my court case."

"I'll follow up your case," she said. "I'm the senior aide to the Kiev City Public Prosecutor. My name is Zoya Karpovna Shevchenko. Well, what a story you have! So you're now a citizen of the U.S.A.?"

"Yes, I am."

"Leave your letter for the public prosecutor with me, and we'll check into your case. When was your trial, and who was the judge?"

"The trial took place in Kiev on January 27-31, 1975. I was tried by the Kiev City Court, with Judge Dyshel presiding. By the way, where is he now? Is he alive?"

"No, Dyshel died several years ago."

"At my trial, he was very spiteful, irritable. . ."

Zoya Karpovna objected. "I think, it only seemed that way. Dyshel was not an evil person by nature. But they made him try you. I'm familiar with the religious cases—all of you were tried not for crimes, but only for ideological reasons. This didn't make it easy for your investigators and judge. They knew that you believers were innocent people, but the KGB was putting great pressure on them. Dyshel did what they told him, although, as I understand, this was against his conscience. I should tell you that Judge Dyshel himself was a very sympathetic, intelligent man."

"Where is investigator Bekh now?" I asked. "He was an investigator not only on my case in 1974, but also on my mother's in 1971. At the time she was 64, when she was tried and sentenced to three years of imprisonment for her faith in God."

"Your mother was also a prisoner?" Zoya Karpovna asked in astonishment.

"Not just my mother. My father, Peter Vins, was arrested in Siberia in 1930 for preaching the Gospel, when I was only two years old. He died in 1943 in a camp in the north in the region of Magadan, on the Kolyma River."

"What a tragic history your family has!" Zoya Karpovna exclaimed. "And where is your mother now?"

"When she was released in December of 1973, she returned to our home in Kiev. When I was exiled, she went to America with my family. During the six years of her life in America, before she died in 1985, my mother was active in speaking on behalf of the persecuted believers at Christian conferences in the USA, Canada, Germany, Holland, Switzerland, and other countries. Her message always was: 'Don't forget the suffering believers in the USSR!' I still wanted to know about investigator Bekh, "Do you know anything about him?"

"Yes, I knew Bekh. He died too," she answered.

"What did you think of him as a person?" Zoya Karpovna did not answer.

"What about prosecutor Dolinsky? He was my accuser in the trial in Kiev. Do you know him?"

"Yes, I know him," she said. "He is retired and lives in Kiev. Dolinsky is planning to go to America; he has relatives there."

I gave Zoya Karpovna my appeal to the Kiev City Public prosecutor. She asked me to call in two weeks, and we parted.

When I called two weeks later, I found out that my case was being handled by the aide of public prosecutor Leonid Mikhailovich Abramenko. I talked to Abramenko, and he said that the question of my rehabilitation had been decided favorably, and I could come and get the document. Once more I entered the familiar building on Kreschatik Street, the policeman looked at my passport, and directed me to the tenth floor.

Leonid Mikhailovich Abramenko was an elderly man. He showed me a long list of names of people who had been recently rehabilitated.

"I've handled the rehabilitation issues for many years," he said. "Here's a list of names that I personally worked on. I studied the documents of their trials, got acquainted with their biographies, and as a result came to the conclusion that all these people were innocent, unlawfully arrested, and convicted. On this list, there are writers, composers, doctors, diplomats, school teachers, university professors, and church ministers. Your name is also on this list. But the difference between them and you is that all of them were rehabilitated posthumously. And today I've been able to hand the rehabilitation document to a man who survived the years of imprisonment. I am very glad to see you alive and rehabilitated! Congratulations."

Tears formed in the eyes of Abramenko. I thanked him for his concern for the innocent people who had been imprisoned. Then he handed me my rehabilitation document.

"You have the right to receive financial compensation for your time as a prisoner," Abramenko informed me. For each month of imprisonment, you are due 2000 Ukrainian rubles. In addition, for your pension, you also have privileges: each year in prison counts as three years of employment. You were in bonds for eight years, so that counts as twenty-four years toward your pension. Furthermore, you also have the right to receive your confiscated property. What was confiscated after your trial in 1975?"

"They took our furniture, including our couch, bed, table, chairs, a bookcase, and also our refrigerator and washing machine."

Abramenko summed up: "All of this is now due back to you in the form of new things."

I thanked Abramenko for his concern. We parted, and I stopped by the office of Zoya Karpovna Shevchenko. She congratulated me on my rehabilitation, and then asked, "Could you locate a Bible for me? I want to read it, but I don't have one."

I promised to get her a Bible. Then she said, "What a pleasant moment this is, that you are finally rehabilitated! I have worked in the prosecution system of Kiev for more than twenty years and remember well the court cases of believers and of human rights activists." Then she looked upward and with great feeling uttered, "Thank You, God, that in all my years here I did not try even one political case, or even one believer!"

"Praise God!" I said after her.

When I returned to the apartment where my wife was waiting for me, I showed her the rehabilitation document and recounted the day's conversations. This rehabilitation was an official renouncement by today's judicial system of the Kiev Court proceedings of 1975, which was important to me, because that trial was not only of me, but of the Bible and our Christian faith. Getting this change of the court's verdict was a triumph for the Gospel!

For decades, thousands of brothers and sisters in the Lord had stood before judges, passed through prisons, and now are rehabilitated. Each document of rehabilitation speaks of the power and justice of our God: "The Lord knoweth the days of the upright: and their inheritance shall be for ever. . . . They shall not be ashamed in the evil time: and in the days of famine they shall be satisfied" (Psalm 37: 18, 19).

I also told Nadia what Abramenko had said about financial

compensation: "Two thousand Ukrainian rubles' compensation for every month spent in bonds. Eight years of bonds makes ninety-six months. Now the exchange rate is 2000 rubles for one dollar. So, I can receive ninety-six dollars for my eight years of prison!"

Nadia laughed. "That's very generous of the Ukrainian authorities! Better not to receive the compensation. Your bonds are more valuable than the money!"

I agreed with her.

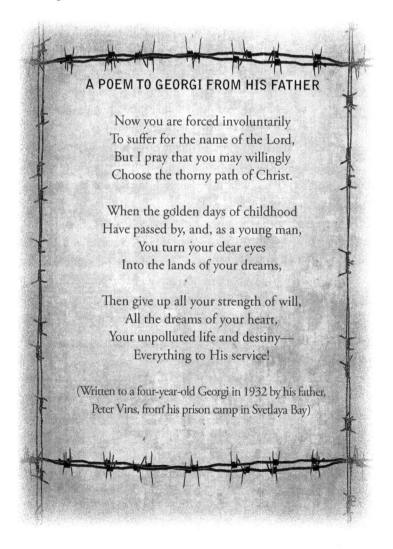

A POEM TO GEORGI FROM HIS FATHER

Now you are forced involuntarily
To suffer for the name of the Lord,
But I pray that you may willingly
Choose the thorny path of Christ.

When the golden days of childhood
Have passed by, and, as a young man,
You turn your clear eyes
Into the lands of your dreams,

Then give up all your strength of will,
All the dreams of your heart,
Your unpolluted life and destiny—
Everything to His service!

(Written to a four-year-old Georgi in 1932 by his father,
Peter Vins, from his prison camp in Svetlaya Bay)

23

NINE TIMES BY 1994

Now, as I am writing this chapter in January of 1994, the temperature has fallen to -27°F. There is so much snow in our small town of Elkhart, Indiana—I'd say we are having a genuine Siberian winter!

In the three years since I first went back to visit my homeland, I have flown from Chicago to Moscow, Kiev, or Khabarovsk nine times, sometimes staying there up to seven weeks. The last time I was in Moscow in October of 1993 during a very difficult time—a veritable war with shooting, fires, murder, tanks on the streets, and a curfew. As I visited believers, we prayed together for protection and help from the Lord. We also prayed for Russia—that God would send a spiritual awakening to the people living in our vast land.

My daughter Natasha and I visited churches in Kazan on the Volga River, where we met believers of the Chuvash nationality. The Lord is awakening the Chuvash people to Christian faith. Two brothers in the church there, Michael and Yuri Trofimov, are accomplished musicians. Yuri, who also is a composer, set several of my poems to music. He said apologetically, "You know, Georgi Petrovich, our Chuvash folk melodies are so plain and simple.

But when Michael and Yuri began playing the piano and singing, what marvelous sounds arose toward heaven, what joy and reverence before our great Lord.

At first they sang in Russian, and then, to my great surprise, they began to sing in Chuvash. I could not listen without tears.

"Who translated my poems into the Chuvash language?" I asked.

"We did," the Trofimov brothers answered. And we all prayed for the spiritual awakening of the 500,000 Chuvash people living in the Volga River Valley.

In Moscow, I had the opportunity to meet with the ministers of the local Baptist church, which had endured much persecution in past years. Today its membership numbers about three hundred. It is a growing church with fifty new believers baptized in 1993 alone. The place where the worship services are held is filled even though it is located outside of Moscow, far from the subway. Getting there by public bus is very difficult, and few believers own cars. For a long time, the Moscow church has wanted to acquire a location within

1984 — GEORGI AND NATASHA SPEAKING IN ALASKA
AT A MISSIONARY CONFERENCE

the city limits. That evening in October 1993 the ministers gathered to discuss this matter. I was also invited. The brothers shared their need, we prayed together, asking the Lord to provide the funds.

With this and other needs for the work of the Gospel in Russia, Ukraine, Belarus, Siberia, and the Far East I returned to America.

Lord! You see the needs of our people in my homeland. Hear the prayer of Your children. I believe that nothing is impossible for you. You Yourself said, "If ye abide in me, and my words abide in you, ye shall ask what ye will, and it shall be done unto you" (John 15:7).

When I returned home from Moscow, my wife said, "How concerned I was for you! I was afraid that someone would shoot you in Moscow during the chaos." We prayed together and thanked the Lord for His protection. I told Nadia that while I was there hundreds of Muscovites were killed, thousands were wounded, but not even one believer was hurt!"

I love Psalm 91 for its very pertinent words: "He that dwelleth in the secret place of the most High shall abide under the shadow of the Almighty. I will say of the Lord, He is my refuge and my fortress: my God; in him will I trust. . . . A thousand shall fall at thy side, and ten thousand at thy right hand; but it shall not come nigh thee" (Psalm 91:1,2,7).

Indeed, the Lord preserves those who trust in Him!

Back home in Elkhart, I recall my trips to Russia and Ukraine over the past three years. Everything has been fast paced, dynamic, and emotional. Due to my open-heart surgery in 1990, my health cannot sustain such a load. I always return to America worn out physically. After every trip, it seems to me that this has been my last one, and that soon, very soon, I will depart for my heavenly homeland. But after a month or so, I get back to normal and start planning another trip.

I realize that the Lord is the One who has widely opened a door for evangelization in my homeland, where one hundred twenty different nationalities dwell. I love not only the Russians and Ukrainians, among whom I spent a major part of my life, but also the Belarusians, Moldovans, Chuvash, Tartars, and many other peoples of the former Soviet Union, including the peoples of Northern Siberia: Yakuts, Evenks, Ukagirs, to whom I witnessed about Christ during my labor camp years in Yakutia.

I rejoice that the Lord is carrying out the great work of spiritual awakening among the peoples of the former Soviet Republics, who for seventy years were taught only atheism and denial of God. How important it is to understand God's strategy in relation to Russia—it's possible this is God's last summons before His glorious coming! Jesus said: "And this gospel of the kingdom shall be preached in all the world for a witness unto all nations: and then shall the end come" (Matthew 24:14).

One question constantly looms before me: what can and must be done to aid the work of the Gospel in the former Soviet Union? How can we make better use of the God-given freedom for preaching the Gospel in the country where state atheism reigned for seventy years? For the last several years, the Lord has given Russian Gospel Ministries the opportunity to send hundreds of thousands of Bibles, Gospels, and other Christian literature to Russia and many other parts of the former Soviet Union. Today, we continue to send Christian literature, thanks to the prayers and financial help of Christian friends in America and Canada.

NADIA AND GEORGI IN 1985

24

MY FIRST POEM, MY FIRST ARREST, AND REVIVAL IN RUSSIA

I was born in Russia's Far East. My father, Peter Vins, was an American missionary who went to Russia in 1926, and since 1927 served as a pastor of an 800-member Evangelical Baptist Church in Blagoveschensk, a city on the Chinese border. There he met and married Lydia Zharikova, a Russian girl, and on August 4, 1928, I was born to them.

In December of 1930, my father was arrested and sentenced to three years of prison camps. (In those years over two hundred members of the Blagoveschensk church were arrested and exiled out of the city.) After his release in 1933, he continued to preach the Gospel. In 1937, he was arrested again and sentenced to ten years of prison camps without rights to visitation and correspondence with his family. On December 27, 1943, at the age of 46, my father died from starvation in a prison camp near Magadan, on the Kolyma River*(see note on bottom of next page).

My childhood memories are filled with constant house searches and arrests of believers. Faith in God was illegal, and believers were sheep for the slaughter, just as it is written: "For thy sake we are killed all the day long; we are accounted as sheep for the slaughter" (Romans 8:36).

I believed in God from my earliest childhood. I loved and respected my parents. I knew they were suffering for Christ and for a spiritual awakening of the Russian people. Even before starting school, I already knew the primer and could read and write, thanks to my mother, who taught me. At six or seven years of age, I began to write poetry—simple children's verses about God, my faith in Him, and my love for Jesus Christ.

When my father was arrested in 1937, my mother and I were left alone. None of our relatives lived in Omsk. I was afraid that the authorities would arrest my mother, and I would be left completely alone. Arrests usually took place late in the evening or at night, so I spent every evening in expectation of her arrest. Each night before going to sleep Mother and I prayed, "Lord, preserve Papa, and defend us. Don't let Mother be arrested . . ."

GEORGI—(7 YEARS OLD)

MY FIRST POEM

I wrote a poem when I was seven—
My first—it was of faith and courage;
But then at night "the knock" proclaimed
A search and, dazed, I could not think
Where to conceal my sheet of paper.

From * on previous page: This is the official information Georgi Vins' mother was given by the Soviet authorities in 1961 after repeated written requests to let her know what happened to her husband. However, that turned out to be false information: when in 1995 Georgi Vins was permitted to see the secret police's prison dossier on his father, he found out that, like many other Christian leaders, his father was shot on August 26, 1937, at the age of 39, in prison in the city Omsk, Siberia.

There came a time of turbulence
That saw our father taken from us.
Siberian night and winter's blast,
Longings for morn to break at last
And joy "the knock" was not repeated.

But I kept writing, and each day
My verse, although so childish—awkward,
Kept springing up; at first a shoot,
And then a blade—into full flower . . .
I ceased to fear the ice land's power.

Since then the decades have marched by.
Life's autumn stands upon the threshold;
But now of Christ, my Lord, I write
Because He is my chief delight
And without *Him* my life is worthless.

I dedicate these lines to those
Who for Christ's truth are battling bravely.
By faith, before them mountains fall
And many heed the Savior's call
Because today to God they're faithful.

And in that final hour I'll say
(Though very likely not in verses)
To Him my words of love and praise,
And endless rhapsody I'll raise
As I'm embraced at last by Heaven.

REVIVAL

At the beginning of the 1960s, the Lord sent a spiritual revival among the Evangelical Baptists[1] of the Soviet Union. The revival preceded a great assault from the atheistic authorities. Soviet newspapers and magazines spewed an endless flow of articles against believers and the Christian faith, against the Bible and God. Radio, television, and movies were used for anti-religious propaganda. Believers were fired from their jobs, and Christian young people were kept out of educational institutions.

In 1960, the Soviet leader, head of the Communist party, Nikita Khrushchev, announced a twenty-year program of definitively creating communism in the Soviet Union. By 1980, there was not to be a single Christian left, nor one church. All citizens of the USSR would have to become atheists and confess only Communist ideology.

In Evangelical Baptist churches, sermons on salvation were forbidden, and children under the age of sixteen were not to be permitted to be present at church services. As a primary measure, it was also forbidden to baptize young people under the age of thirty. This decision of the leadership of the Communist Party of the Soviet Union was enforced by the KGB, the police, and other authorities.

Unfortunately, some of the ministers of Evangelical Baptist churches, fearing persecution, accepted these ungodly decrees as the basis for their ministry and actively began to implement them in the church. The churches were going through great testings. Many thousands of believers raised their voices in fervent prayer to the Lord for help and deliverance. The Lord heard those prayers and answered His people, as it is written in His Word: "It is time for thee, Lord, to work: for they have made void thy law" (Psalm 119:126).

A spiritual awakening began. New churches started to take shape, and groups of believers who refused to compromise with atheism proclaimed the Word of God as the absolute authority in all matters of faith and life. Young people and children attended newly formed congregations whose worship services often took place in crowded private homes or in forests. These meetings were subject to cruel disruption by the KGB and police, with the police beating up believers, and throwing them out of the meeting houses into the snow. Bulldozers were sometimes used to destroy the places where the meetings took place.

The atheistic authorities went to believers' work places with threats of arrests and trials. But no one could stop the revival, because the Word of God says, "Who shall separate us from the love of Christ? shall tribulation, or distress, or persecution, or famine, or nakedness, or peril, or sword? As it is written, For thy sake we are killed all the day long; we are accounted as sheep for the slaughter. Nay, in all these things we are more than conquerors through him that loved us" (Romans 8:35-37).

By 1966, several hundred independent fundamental Baptist churches had formed. Sixty to seventy percent of the membership of these churches were young people between the ages of fifteen and thirty. The hearts of believers burned with great love toward God, courage, and selflessness in ministry. My poem "Revival" was written in January of 1966, and five months later, in May of 1966, I was arrested in Moscow for taking part in the revival.

> My Savior! How I love Your precious call
> To slaves of unbelief, by sin defeated.
> You long to bless and have each one delight
> In all the joys of our eternal promise.
>
> My Jesus! Mighty is Your matchless love,
> Your hands are full of tenderness and kindness,
> As constantly You lift to life anew
> The sons of earth, to save them from destruction.
>
> Our brethren You have visited once more
> With Your pure flame of heaven-sent revival!
> For exploits and for suff'ring You inspired
> To stand for truth and infinite salvation.
>
> When I behold the vibrant Christian youth
> With glowing faces, joyous and exultant,
> Their gladness like a boundless ocean's tide,
> Burst forth in ever glorious songs of triumph. . . .

And when I listen to a youthful soul
For the first time, his heart to God uplifting:
Scarce breathing then I reverently pray,
While in my thoughts the sufferers recalling. . . .

I know that not in vain their blood was spilt!
They did not bear the pain and grief for nothing.
For now I see our youth's pure, fervent love
Their hands stretched out to Christ in supplication.

For the revival burning in our church
And for our youth rejoicing in the Savior—
We may, without misgivings or dismay,
Lay down our very lives in distant prisons.

January 1, 1966
Kiev

TO MOTHER

When I was arrested for my Christian ministry in 1966, I was thirty-eight. From the time of my father's arrest in Stalin's time to my own arrest, thirty years had passed. But faith in God was still considered just as dangerous to the government. Believers still endured arrests, prisons, house raids and searches, and the confiscation of Bibles, religious literature, and even personal letters mentioning God.

I was arrested in Moscow on May 19, 1966, and put in Lefortovo, Moscow's main KGB prison. Behind me remained freedom, my family, and friends. My wife Nadia, our four children, and my mother Lydia lived in Kiev, Ukraine. Just a month before my arrest, my youngest daughter, Jane, had taken her first step. Now this was a first step for me, too, but to prison. The heavy metal cell door slammed shut. When would I again see my wife, children, and dear elderly mother? My world narrowed to four stone walls with a sturdy iron door. The prison window was enclosed by a double grating. Beyond the window, it was springtime, with an expanse of sky and spacious fields, but my cell was a silent stone grave, where enemies of the Gospel constantly tried to enslave my soul, to humiliate and break me. Through a small, hinged pane of glass in the window, I could see a bit of rainy sky. It looked like the sky was crying. *Is it not for us, the Christian prisoners, confined to the gloomy walls of an old Russian prison?* I wondered.

At first, I was held alone, in a solitary cell. After three days, guards transferred me to a cell where there was another prisoner, arrested for serious financial crimes. I paced around my cell: six feet forward, six feet back. My thoughts turned to my family, and toward Jesus Christ, the Savior of the world, who gives genuine freedom, happiness, and the power to resist atheism. I also thought of my brothers in Christ in the neighboring cells. Even in the midst of prison walls our great God strengthened our faith and inspired bright hope in our hearts. Christ is invincible! Faith lives and grows stronger.

Days, weeks, and months pass slowly for prisoners. Despite the strict isolation of Lefortovo prison, the captive Christians were able, bit by bit, to establish contact with each other through other prisoners. By August, I had news about most of my friends held in Lefortovo prison. They were in good spirits and firm in their commitment to God. Some had already been tried and had had a meeting with their families after the trial. Through them I learned that my loved ones were well and that my mother had come to Moscow to be present at several trials. The word was passed to me that she looked very sad. Sweet mother! Once again, prison had visited us. *Since 1930 when you were only 23, your life has passed under the shadow of prisons and camps: first the imprisonment of your husband, and now—your son. You have borne many trials on the thorny path of Russian Christians. But don't be sad! Christ is the Victor over death and hell, and how much more over modern atheism!* In my cell in Lefortovo, I wrote a poem dedicated to my mother.

> I hear that you have been grieving,
> Mother, so dear to my heart,
> Prison once more has intruded
> Tearing our family apart.

Throughout your youth: constant journeys
Father in prison, exile,
You walked more closely with Jesus
Facing each test, ev'ry mile.

Life poses difficult problems—
Losses so heavy to bear . . .
Still you are visiting prisons,
But it's your son who is there.

Do not despair, my beloved!
Trust in the victory of Christ!
Our great millennium is glowing
Immortal triumph of Christ.

From ev'ry sorrow, each martyr,
Fruit more abundant will spring:
Strength will increase without measure,
Many new conqu'rors will bring.

LYDIA VINS IN 1985—ELKHART, INDIANA. SHE WORKED UNTIL THE
END OF HER LIFE TO HELP PERSECUTED CHRISTIANS IN THE U.S.S.R.

25

PRISON POEMS AND THE STORIES BEHIND THEM

FREEDOM IS NOT FOR IDLENESS

I served my three-year term of imprisonment in the northern Urals. In May of 1969, I was approaching the end of my term. Soon I'd be going home. The camp officers tried to frighten me: "A directive from Moscow could give you a new term of imprisonment!" They were constantly warning me that if I got released, walked out the gate, and talked to anyone about faith in God, they would arrest me again right there before I even got home. And if I did reach home, they said, I should keep quiet and not preach or even visit church services, or I would end up in prison again. I asked the Lord for strength to remain faithful to Him.

Freedom is ahead! But for what? To refrain from preaching the Gospel? To live under the constant fear of a new arrest? The Russian people need Christ! I could not keep silent about God's love toward people. Our Lord Jesus Christ said, "Greater love hath no man than this, that a man lay down his life for his friends" (John 15:13). No, the Lord was giving me freedom for a new ministry in the vast mission field of Russia. My last poem written in a Ural mountain labor camp was "Freedom Is Not for Idleness!"

For idleness, we don't desire freedom,
A holy labor waits in virgin soil!
The melting, ringing song of spring is sounding
And harvest fields are rousing from their sleep.

The holy morning of Christ's Resurrection
Fills with abundant strength and thrills our breast!
Once more the message of the Gospel's sounding
Of Him, the One who wakens souls to life.

The persecuted churches meet with gladness!
In many eyes, there glisten tears of joy,
And to our God a gratitude, unending,
Glows with a flaming love in every heart.

My friends, I know how harsh has been the pathway
You passed along, in heavy chains for Christ!
Today you still untremblingly are willing
To walk in far-off places for the Faith.

For idleness, we don't desire freedom!
We have been called the good news to proclaim,
To serve our people still must be our purpose,
To serve our God—our honor and delight!

April 1969
The Urals, Anyusha Prison Camp

RESURRECTION'S DAWN

The northern Urals are beautiful in both winter and summer with endless wooded expanses, numerous picturesque rivers, and low mountains. Winters there are long; snow covers the ground for up to half a year, the temperature generally is about -4° or -22°F, but there are days and even weeks when the temperature drops to -58°, and even as low as -83°. Then life seems to freeze. In the forest, all is still and windless: you don't see any birds or animals, just blindingly white snow, and plenty of it. Snowdrifts can be six feet high, so deep that in the villages and settlements you can see only the roofs of the houses or chimneys sticking out of unbroken snowy flatness.

Winters in the northern Urals are beautiful, but for prisoners the snowy winter doles out great misery, since they must fell trees in the woods. We had to clear away the snow from each tree, then saw the tree, and after this use an axe to lop off the branches and twigs from the trunk, which had fallen into deep snow. Then the prisoners must

THE URAL MOUNTAINS, RUSSIA

carry it out on their shoulders, again through snow three feet deep. While working, we were cold and hungry due to the poor clothing and very meager food. Around us stood guards, armed soldiers, and dogs. The route of two miles from the camp to the work site in the woods was difficult, and we had to walk at a fast pace. That's the way it was every morning. But it was especially hard to come back to the cold, unheated barracks of the camp after working outside all day.

In late April and May comes the long-awaited spring. The good, gentle sun warms so tenderly. The snow thins and melts. The running brooks babble cheerfully all around. On the hillsides appear bright green blades of grass and the first fragile flowers of spring—snow-white snowdrops. Powerful spruce trees and fir trees lightly sway their branches, freeing themselves of the snow. Thawed rivers and streams also break loose from their frozen cloaks, often overflowing their banks, and noisily race toward the south.

Awakening from winter's hibernation, the taiga comes to life as the sun sends out its life-giving rays. People, too, seem to awaken from the icy breath of the north to life, warmth, and gladness.

But for us believers, spring is a reminder of the soul's resurrection from the mire of sin and unbelief, from hopelessness to life, to the only Source of life— Jesus Christ, who said, "I am the resurrection and the life" (John 11:25). "Wherefore he saith, Awake thou that sleepest, and arise from the dead, and Christ shall give thee light" (Eph. 5:14). The Word of God thus calls to all people.

> Brooks rush pell-mell and forests throb with birdsong,
> As Spring comes flying on the crane's strong wings.
> And tenderly from skies of deepest azure
> Stream ever warmer rays of golden sun.
>
> I love the Spring—a symbol of revival
> From Winter's sleep of darkness, unbelief. . . .
> Just as a pris'ner, leaving cell so gloomy,
> Speeds with a joyful vigor to the light.

So many times I ponder about Christ,
Of all the awful depths of Calvary's suff'ring:
Harsh nakedness veiled only by His blood,
There, He was dying for creation fallen.

Oh, how the evil, crafty enemy
Wished to destroy by death the Truth so holy,
Increase sin to a magnitude unheard of
And plunge the universe into despair.

But He arose!
And it was in the Springtime . . .
The rivers leap, the woods exult with joy,
And o'er the earth resounds a shout of vict'ry:
Christ now is risen!
Yes, He's risen indeed!

And, Oh, my Russia! Greet the Resurrection.
At break of day arise and join the song!
Only in Christ your soul will find salvation,
For only He is Light and Truth and Life!

Yakutia, Tabaga Prison Camp
1977

CHILDREN, MY CHILDREN

This poem was written in Kiev Prison, where I was transported after my second arrest in Novosibirsk on March 31, 1974.

Oh, my children, my children! Again years of parting...
Through the walls of my cell, I can still see your eyes,
Your sweet, innocent faces and soft, clinging fingers—
And your lashes that glisten with tears.

How can I comfort you in our time of brief visit?
Should I say that when I was a boy only seven
And I parted from father, I choked down my sobbing,
Then saw only his picture for all these long years?

Should I tell you of this, that throughout all the trials
I have loved with my whole heart our vast spreading land;
The colorful threads of the northern lights dancing,
And my native Ukraine's dreaming woodlands and fields?

Oh, my children, my children! To you I'm bequeathing
Faith and Truth, Love of God—these give meaning to life!
My whole heart longs to live every day with my Savior,
Then—the limitless blue of my heavenly land!

Kiev, Lukyanovskaya Prison
1974

THE HILLS HAVE WRAPPED THEMSELVES IN GLOOMY VAPORS

This poem was written in the autumn of 1976 in the Yakut prison camp called "Tabaga," where I was sent from Kiev after being sentenced to five years of strict-regime labor camp and five years of exile.

The Tabaga camp is located in northern Siberia, some six thousand miles from my family in Kiev. Over a year had passed since my arrest, and many more years of imprisonment still lay ahead. A Siberian autumn of gloomy fogs and depressing rains began. It became so lonely and dreary... *The hills have wrapped themselves in gloomy vapors, And dismal rains are weaving sadness there* . . . Thus a new poem began to be born. But somewhere chestnut trees are gilt by sunshine. But don't wait for a meeting with them!

Don't wait for release and a meeting with loved ones! Ahead lie many more years of imprisonment, and then five years of Siberian exile. However, after the first stanza the verse didn't move forward. I kept thinking: "Don't wait! Your destiny is only prison camp, gloomy vapors, and depressing rains—that's all. Loneliness, hardships, dejection—there is all your lot . . ." The poem remained unfinished and would not unwind any further: there was nothing else to say. Despair! An impasse!

"But what about faith? What about hoping in the Lord?!" I began to question myself. "And we know that all things work together for good to them that love God, to them who are the called according to his purpose" (Romans 8:28). How could I let this wonderful verse from the Scriptures slip from my mind? And suddenly, like a bolt of lightning, a joyful thought lit up my soul: "*Have hope! And faith! Keep waiting! Don't despair!*" And so a whole stanza had poured itself out:

The hills have wrapped themselves in gloomy vapors,
And dismal rains are weaving sadness there..
But somewhere chestnut trees are gilt by sunshine..
Have hope!
  And faith!
    Keep waiting!
      Don't despair!

For those with faith, all things will bring some blessing:
The rains of autumn, even winter's gales!
Flash floods of spring rampaging down the gullies,
And flowers of May full-blooming in the dales.

For those who love there's access to perfection
In holy patience and in faithfulness,
Possessing inner peace unshakable
And blessedness of joy that is unending!

Yakutia, Tabaga Prison Camp
1976

MY PRISON SONG

In the Tabaga prison camp, I worked as an electrician in the saw mill. At my workplace in the electrical room, I planted a flower in a jar. I carefully tended it: I watered it and put it at the window to be nearer the light. However, in the camp we often experienced water shortages when there would not be enough water even for drinking. Then I shared my portion of water with the flower. Finally, the flower put forth tender bright-red petals.

Once I brought a hungry kitten with a broken tail into my work room. I sheltered it in the electrical room, fed it with bread from my rations and camp soup, which I carried out of the camp dining hall in a tin can. On cold winter days the electrical room was a place of rest and warmth for many prisoners, especially for Yakuts, who worked in the snow unloading logs. In my workroom, I was able to have many heart-to-heart spontaneous conversations about faith and God with different prisoners.

Drops of water I've shared with a flower,
Prison bread—with a small, starving kitten,
To a grey-headed man—gave a shirt
That I kept in my prisoner's knapsack.

Labor camp did not padlock my soul:
But, rejecting the law of the wolf pack,
I would share all the warmth of my thoughts
With the downtrodden and the despised ones.

I'll be fifty years old very soon,
An old man, they're beginning to call me.
My days fly as though carried by deer
O'er this far-flung Yakutian region.

The familiar scenes I recall:
Youth's bright morning, the heat of the summer.
But this prisoner song I now sing
To its last verse has not been completed.

And how many more years lie ahead
In the convoys and cells dark and narrow?
Oh, my Jesus, You led, lead me still
Through the storms—to my Heavenly homeland!

Yakutia, Tabaga Prison Camp
1977

PRISON HOSPITAL

In 1977, my health worsened. My heart began having problems and I was hospitalized. Without the proper equipment for checking the heart, all that the doctors could do was take my blood pressure and give some medication. Actually, the most effective treatment in the hospital was having rest and quiet. Even though the hospital was situated in a prison camp, there were no guards inside the hospital. The doctors willingly and conscientiously tried to help us prisoners in whatever way possible. They knew that the conditions of camp life sapped our health. The doctors told me, "You need rest in your condition and absolutely must not get excited."

I already knew this, but it was very hard when the KGB didn't allow me to have letters from my family, or when they incited other prisoners against me and were following my every step. But the Lord sent peace to my heart, as His Word says, "Fear thou not; for I am with thee: be not dismayed; for I am thy God: I will strengthen thee; yea, I will help thee; yea, I will uphold thee with the right hand of my righteousness" (Isaiah 41:10-11). In Psalm 23, David said, "Yea, though I walk through the valley of the shadow of death, I will fear no evil: for thou art with me. . . ." (Psalm 23:4).

Our health, life, and all our future are in the Lord's hands. I very much wanted to be free again, to see the faces of friends and loved ones, and to be in worship services in my own church. I spent more than a month in that prison hospital, where I wrote this poem:

"*Yea, though I walk through the valley of the shadow of death, I will fear no evil: for Thou art with me*" (Psalm 23:4).
Silence reigns . . . a hospital in prison.
Why are you so fearful, Oh, my heart?
Can it be we'll never pray together
As before, where sings the youth of Christ?

They are saying: to Kiev's assembly
Many brand-new brothers, sisters, come
Precious Lord, before I leave forever
How I long to see their flaming joy!

Let me only . . .
   somehow, all unnoticed
Lean my weary heart against the door,
Once again to hear of Christ the Savior
And His Truth that lives forevermore!

Yakutsk, Prison Hospital
Summer 1977

DON'T RUSH TOMORROW

In the camp, I once came across a magazine with an article about the famous German composer Johann Sebastian Bach, who lived in the eighteenth century. This article mentioned Bach's favorite expression: "God's timing is the only true timing!" This phrase brought me great encouragement. The Lord has definite plans for every person who trusts Him. God determines the time of His deeds in each of our lives. I knew that He Himself would determine when to give me freedom.

In 1978, I wrote the poem, "Don't Rush Tomorrow," meaning, don't worry, don't get agitated; consider everything according to God's will. This poem was written as a message to myself. I had no idea then that the day of my release would come unexpectedly. The Lord had already determined all that. My part was to live day by day trusting Him. Right here, at my prison camp, I was not forsaken by the Lord: I had my daily bread, a place to sleep, and most important—the love of Christ, to encourage, defend, and inspire me.

Don't rush tomorrow; for the day will come
Before you know. . . It is ordained by Heaven!
Of bread I have my daily needed portion,
On rainy days I've shelter for my head.

So though my flesh decline and daily weakens,
From exiles long my heart's strong rhythm grows faint,
But still the spirit burns with sacred fire
Without a shade of wav'ring or complaint!

But best of all—the light of Jesus' love,
That pierces every age and generation,
On mighty wings of trust and steady patience
Bears up my soul to radiant victory!

Yakutia, Tabaga Prison Camp
1978

OBSTACLES

The Christian life is a constant spiritual struggle against the powers of evil and unbelief. But with God's help believers can overcome all the numerous obstacles. As Satan attempts to shake and destroy Christian faith, to turn believers away from God, he uses not only prisons and open persecution, but also the seduction of praise, riches, and false teachings. How important it is to not depart from the narrow Christian path, compromising with the devil.

In his day, the Apostle Paul said, "But none of these things move me, neither count I my life dear unto myself, so that I might finish my course with joy, and the ministry, which I have received of the Lord Jesus . . ." (Acts 20:24). "I can do all things through Christ which strengtheneth me" (Philippians 4:13).

Very often upon my life's journey
Obstacles like mountains would arise
Sealing off the expanses of heaven
And my pathway that leads to the skies.

Storms shrieked of death and destruction
And there seemed no appeasing their lust;
Then I heard, from those pages so sacred,
Whispers, "Trust" and again, "Only trust!"

In the midst of the tempest's fierce howling
When the tumult was too much to bear,
From His Word I would hear God's voice speaking,
"You'll find power though prayer—yes, through prayer!"

So I trusted and walked on unswerving,
And to quiet the storm I would pray;
Then the mountains obstructing my pathway
Meekly trembled and faded away.

O the Bible—God's good news from heaven,
A celestial, inspired melody;
I don't know of a Book more amazing
And how precious its song is to me!

1987

WE HAVE LEFT OUR NATIVE LAND

My five-year sentence of imprisonment in strict-regime camp ended on March 31, 1979. Five more years of internal exile still lay in store for me. My place of exile had been designated as a distant northern region of Tyumenskaya oblast, in a swampy, almost unpopulated area. But rather than exile in that rotten place, I was transferred by convoy to Moscow, where I was informed of a decision by the Supreme Soviet of the USSR that I was to be deprived of my Soviet citizenship and expelled from the country. Thus, on April 27, 1979, I was transported under guard from Moscow on the Aeroflot jet to the United States of America.

At Kennedy Airport in New York City, five of us former Soviet prisoners were exchanged for two Soviet spies who had been caught in America and sentenced to fifty years each. My comrades in freedom were former political prisoners. I was the only one of us who had been in bonds for Christian faith.

We were departing from our native land
Not of our own free wills, most certainly.
Pain clutched our hearts—constricting, searing.
A rain-swept runway, and the moment nearing
When Moscow whispers finally, "Farewell!"

The ever-present convoy's on the plane
With the same air of arrogance and coldness.

And I—a pris'ner, now without a country—
Still seeing labor camps, so dark and hungry,
Still hearing howls, the angry guard-dog howls.

But I was praying for my enemies...
I asked for meekness and for full submission,
A heart that's pure and undepraved by harshness.
I thanked the Lord for long and needed patience
That He had sent to me through terms in bonds.

Years passed, and all about is strange and new.
The road back to my home is barricaded.
My enemies are still unsatiated
Their hearts still filled with hatred unabated,
And slander never ceases from their lips.

But now I pray and wait. My native land
Shall hunger for the truth—Christ's blessed teachings,
And she will say, "My soul is ready now, Lord,
To hear and to accept Your saving love;
Your Word brings hope and peace from heaven above."

1987

FREEDOM

This poem reflects my impressions of those first hours of freedom on American soil: such an unexpected freedom, but also pain from parting with friends in Christ and my homeland Russia. The joy of freedom and the bitterness of separation, concern for the persecuted friends back home—these were the feelings that overflowed my heart in the first hours of freedom.

First hours in New York City,
First gulp of absolute freedom.
Still tasting bitter parting
For years . . . it may be, many years.

Hotel luxurious, first class,
Swarming reporters. . . people...
Freedom crashed down without warning,
Like a volley of thousands of cannons.

But I'm still in yesterday's world:
Out of my memory keep rising
Convoys, Siberian prisons,
The labor camp cold in Yakutia...

I can see: brethren tormented,
Thrust once again into prisons.
To the whole world I'm proclaiming:
"This is for faith in Christ Jesus!"

New York
April 28, 1979

PILGRIM

In November 1986, I visited England, Northern Ireland, and Scotland, where I was able to preach in churches and at Christian conferences. As I did everywhere, I appealed to believers in Great Britain to prayerfully support the persecuted believers in my homeland. In England, the Lord gave me the opportunity to visit the places where John Bunyan had preached the Gospel in the seventeenth century and where he spent twelve years in bonds for his faith. I was able to visit the John Bunyan museum in Bedford, where the door to his prison is still preserved. Russian believers love John Bunyan's books *Pilgrim's Progress* and *The Holy War*. For them, it is special that John Bunyan was faithful to God and witnessed of His love, despite the prohibitions of the authorities of that far-off time.

There's a land—among lands—stands forth,
Though so often by mists it's enveloped;
Land of isles set in grey ocean waves.
It is here that I met with John Bunyan!

And I walked in the places he knew,
Saw the door of his desolate prison;
Understanding (though centuries have passed)
Pilgrim's essence, while reading his story.

Pilgrim's journey—how hard his path
And how crafty the forces against him!
Oft his pain-weary heart almost failed;
All around him were graves of the conquered.

Many fearful, in dread, turned back;
Many, weakened by sin, were defeated.
Only Faith had the power to withstand
And before Faith alone heaven opened!

Hedged by thorns is the Christian's road;
On it many dear brethren have suffered.
Here it was that John Bunyan once trod
As he published the love of our Savior.

MY DAUGHTER HAS GONE BACK TO RUSSIA

In 1988, my daughter Natasha was granted a visa from the Soviet embassy for a two-week visit to Moscow, Leningrad, Kiev, and Kharkov. This was a big event not only in Natasha's life but also in the life of our whole family. For the first time since my exile in 1979, a member of our family had an opportunity to go back to our homeland. On May 29, 1988, I drove Natasha to O'Hare Airport in Chicago. We prayed together, and she went to board the airplane to Moscow. I described my feelings concerning this trip in the poem "My Daughter Has Gone Back to Russia."

Far away, across the vast blue ocean,
Thresholds of my past, my native land . . .
And my daughter's traveling to Russia—
For two weeks, so very brief a time.

Once again she'll hear songs of revival,
About Christ in our own native tongue,
Be with friends—she'll grasp each precious moment
To be ever treasured in her soul.

As your father, now I give my blessing
Praying to the Lord in humbleness,
That He will protect you, my beloved,
So you'll see once more our land of Rus!

See again the peaceful morning breaking,
And the bridges over Neva bright...
Give to all my warmest, heartfelt greetings—
All whose souls are faithful to the Lord.

Once again, I trust, you will be with them
In their humble forest meeting place,
Where the love of Christ is their foundation. .
This good news I carry everywhere.

In Ukraine give to our friends this message,
That our bond of brotherhood I keep:
Through the Son of God united always,
He has made us one through His shed blood.

I believe the Lord can hear and answer,
He will make reality from dreams...
Higher than the birds, above clouds rising
Goes your plane into the distant blue.

Chicago
May 29, 1988

ON THE DEATH OF MY MOTHER

On a sunny Sunday morning, May 19, 1985, at 6:45 a.m., my dear mother Lydia, at the age of 78, departed for her eternal dwelling with God. But exactly one week before that, on May 12, our family had celebrated Mother's Day with her. Mother was very lively that day. She seemed so happy surrounded by her loved ones, and neither she nor we knew that by the next Sunday she would be in a heavenly gathering of the saints, in the presence of her greatly beloved Savior Jesus Christ.

Of course for me, as her son, it was hard to accept that she was no longer with us. But faith in God and the bright hope of meeting with her at the feet of Christ gives strength and courage to bear such a sudden separation.

My mother was precious to more than just our family. Many Christian prisoners and their families loved her, as did many other believers in the USSR, because her heart was always with those who were persecuted for Christ's sake. In her own life, she also walked the path of suffering, but remained faithful to God. I want to quote from a letter she sent me in 1967, when I was in a prison camp in the northern Urals:

My dearest son,

A big hug to you! How is your health? In my thoughts, I've talked to you often and am full of anxiety, but just haven't written. I received your precious letter. It was a comfort for my old years. How often we do not understand elderly people—their frailties and their love. But after they are gone, everything comes to remembrance and grieves us. One way or another, everyone comes into this world in order to walk his path and then depart.

But the main thing is how one walks. The honorable way is difficult. I'm not just talking about financial honesty, but about spiritual integrity, so as to walk straight without bending the soul or seeking only personal advantage. Many have gone down this hard road, but compared to the general masses, they are few. They are admired more after their death, but while alive they are considered 'strange' by people with lower standards.

The spirit and motto of our days is "Take everything you can from life!" But in following this principle people get burned very quickly, and like butterflies scorch their wings in the flame and become groveling and disparaged, spending their remaining years misshapen and ruined.

Your path is hard. I know there are bitter minutes of loneliness when it seems like you're falling under the weight of the cross. Don't faint. Behind the clouds, the sun is shining! You're still young, only 39. Lord willing, you'll survive and even forget these sufferings. You'll just carry the lessons for all of your life. It's good to gain the godly quality of knowing how to be patient and meek even when men attack that which is most precious and noble in your soul. This is one of the most essential things in life. However, I am not talking about the groveling of a slave, because in such a case a person's worthiness and the pursuit of eternal life lose themselves.

I'd like to tell you much about our life with all its afflictions and joys, but not this time. Everything is all right with us. The gardens have bloomed. The days are flying forward, and we're flying with them. What are we taking with us? As it is written, "Their works do follow them" (Revelation 14:13). The years will pass really fast. You will come home, hug everyone again, and once more, the joys of freedom will be yours.

May God be with you! Amidst

Lydia (1907-1985)

all misfortunes, may He preserve your heart from bitterness, and may your life be secured in full safety. I constantly pray for you and entrust you to Him, the Guardian of our souls! We will lay our hope on Him, our breath and life are in His hands.

Your mother

During the first weeks after her death, I wrote:

"ON THE DEATH OF MY MOTHER"

Suddenly, you left us for God's homeland
On a Sunday as the day was born,
And beyond the river stood in wonder
In the springtime brightness of that morn.

Here, the birds were gladly warbling May songs
And the flow'rs were waking—tremblingly;
Gentle breezes, blades of grass caressing,
Quivered in still drowsy shrubbery.

You alone are silent, unresponsive
To the beauty so familiar here.
You're beholding something far more cherished
Something that's become more loved and near.

Gates of Paradise for you have opened!
Thousands of your friends you now can see
Praising God with songs of joyful triumph,
For salvation from earth's misery.

MY JESUS

It is fascinating to study the history of mankind and examine men's attempts to get by without God, which brings constant tragic mistakes and errors. Comparing it all with who Jesus Christ is, a believer is once again in deep reverence and amazement, persuaded of the immeasurable wisdom of God. In the Bible, we find the depth of the teaching of Christ and the beauty of His divine character. An even greater desire to imitate Christ rises in our hearts, as it is written: "Let this mind be in you, which was also in Christ Jesus" (Philippians 2:5).

> You bore the enmity and fierce reviling
> Of evil men with hearts honed sharp by hate,
> For Your redeeming work, the narrow pathway,
> My Jesus, Savior and Creator great!

> And those who yesterday proclaimed, "Hosanna!"
> As loudly clamor for our death today.
> They cannot understand Your soul's deep sorrow,
> Your tears for those who perish on the way.

> You became Conqueror by love and meekness.
> In faithfulness unto a heavenly call
> You trampled Death, and by Your resurrection
> Revealed the greatest miracle of all.

> Lord, I would walk today along Your pathway
> Undaunted by the slander or the sneer.
> O help me with a soul unspotted, like You
> To face the enemy and never fear.

CAN IT BE?

On August 15, 1990, Soviet President Mikhail Gorbachev reversed the decree of the Supreme Soviet by which I had been stripped of my Soviet citizenship and exiled from my homeland.

Now, after eleven years of separation, I was able to go back again. However, two months before that, in June of 1990 I had suffered a severe heart attack followed by open-heart surgery. So, the news that the door to Russia was once again opened to me, I received while recovering after the operation. I greatly rejoiced and thanked the Lord for providing this opportunity. However, when I asked my surgeon about traveling there, his answer was, "Not until a year after the surgery, which would be in June of 1991."

My surgeon, Dr. Ish, is a Christian. Before the operation, he had prayed with me and my family and said, "I believe that the Lord will mend your heart, and you will be able to visit your friends in Russia again."

When two months after the surgery I went back for a check-up, I reminded Dr. Ish of his words, and said, "I would like to go to Russia in November of this year."

"This is way too soon," he replied. "Your heart may not stand the flight across the ocean, and the stress will add pressure."

"What about going by faith?" I asked.

"Well, if you do it by faith, you can go," the doctor finally agreed.

My wife and I applied for a visa. While waiting for the final arrangements, I wrote the poem "Can It Be?" The last part of the poem was written in Leningrad, after I arrived in Russia.

Can it be that I soon will be seeing
My dear brothers and sisters again?
Can it be that once more I'll be hearing
Russian choirs singing songs about Christ?

In the language familiar since childhood
I will hear and drink in God's own Word!
And my heart is prepared for this gladness,
I had dreamed of it while far away.

Years have flown . . . as the birds in migration
Swiftly speed with sad cries to the south;
But how strong were the walls of my prison
Bound by chains—bitter dread and farewells.

After that, the great waves of the ocean
Thrust the coast of my homeland away . . .
And each day, like a craft small and lonely,
Was besprinkled by sorrowful tears.

The afflictions groaned on without number
As the waves of destruction rose high.
Only faith through the clouds shone more brightly,
And the Lord strengthened me by His love.

But today, with great joy I am seeing
My dear brothers and sisters again!
And I hardly dare breathe, as I'm hearing
Russian choirs singing songs about Christ!

I am listening once more to God's message,
Once again with the brethren I pray.
Oh, how precious to me are Christ's people
And a Russia that seeks God today!

Elkhart-Leningrad
November 1990

LENINGRAD, USSR—CIRCA 1962

ALL WAS TAKEN AWAY

Seventy years of an atheistic, anti-God government in Russia left a strong imprint on the life and philosophy of our people. Atheism took away people's faith in God and the Bible, took away their understanding of integrity, goodness, mercy, and compassion. The atheists cultivated a cult of social class struggle, violence, murder, hostility, and cruelty. A spiritual awakening is the only way out from the dead-end that our people have ended up in. They need a decisive turn to God and Jesus Christ. The poems written in September of 1991, "All Was Taken Away," and "Christ and Russia," are dedicated to this theme.

They stole away the soul of Russia,
The surge to kindness and compassion.
And now the toxic rains of fallout—
Chernobyl's awful retribution.

They took away hope's radiant splendor
And faith was locked away in prison . . .
While truth's unsullied snowy garments
Were cast onto the filth of trash heaps.

That was a time of alienation
From faith and every sense of mercy.
The foe, with fierce and blatant vigor,
Sowed seeds of coarse and brutal harshness.

The nation reeled in deep confusion,
Pollution poisoned lakes and rivers . . .
But for my native land, its people,
I'm praying for a resurrection.

Moscow
September 1991

GEORGI VINS

CHRIST AND RUSSIA

Russia and flowers, Russia and poetry—
Does it not sound a little strange to you?
And how can we forget the wrongs and all the sins,
The grief, and shame, that time unprecedented?!

Russia and goodness, Russia and Christ—
Path of new birth, and tears of repentance.
And mercy—not merely in the realm of dreams,
But of the very highest heavenly calling.

Russia, don't plunge into a bottomless abyss,
Think of your sons and all your future grandsons.
Christ Jesus shed His precious blood for you!
Yes, for your sake He bore the awful suffering!

Apart from God there is no way, there is no life—
Only a gloomy, miserable existence.
In Christ is love and truth and glorious light,
Eternity's most holy sure foundation.

Russia and Christ!
       Russia for Christ!
This is my love, my prayer, and expectation!
It was for this so many walked the distant road
Through icy arctic breath of countless prisons.

My Russia! Native land! 0, how can I explain
The love of Christ to you, His great longsuffering?!
Arise and live! You're meant for fellowship with God!
Accept Christ Jesus and obtain salvation!

September 1991
Moscow

EPILOGUE

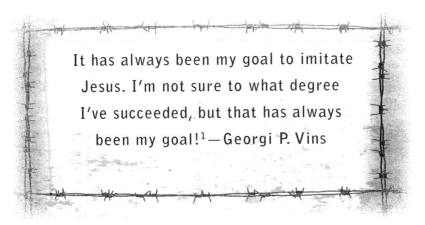

It has always been my goal to imitate
Jesus. I'm not sure to what degree
I've succeeded, but that has always
been my goal![1] — Georgi P. Vins

GEORGI VINS served a total of eight years in prison for his faith.
Halfway through his final ten-year term, he was suddenly transferred
from Siberia to a prison in Moscow. On April 27, 1979, he was
stripped of Soviet citizenship and exiled to the United States along
with four other prisoners. The Carter administration had negotiated
to exchange two captured Soviet spies for these prisoners of conscience. Later, Georgi's family was permitted to join him.

Unexpectedly finding himself in America, Georgi immediately
began speaking out and sharing what he knew about the persecution of Christians in the USSR. He founded a Christian ministry
called International Representation to represent, defend, and aid the
persecuted church in the Soviet Union. To this end, he spoke and
preached across North America, South America, Europe, and Aus-
tralia. Wherever people would listen, he shared news of their plight
and requested prayer until the last Baptist prisoner was released in
December 1988. At that point, his renamed mission, Russian Gospel
Ministries (RGM), refocused its efforts on aiding local churches in
their efforts to evangelize their countrymen. RGM began printing
and delivering Scriptures, translating commentaries and other edifying books, collecting funds for church building projects, financially

supporting pastors, contributing toward Christian children's camps, and coordinating educational seminars for pastors.

Then in 1990, Mikhail Gorbachev retracted the decree exiling Georgi Vins from Russia. During the next seven years of his life, Georgi made numerous trips to his homeland where he preached at churches, schools, colleges, prisons, and open-air street meetings. One of his great joys was seeing the influx of countless new believers at services and the planting of new churches. From 1996 to 1997, he made some of his longest trips deep into Russia, where he visited the site of a labor camp where he had once been held and learned that a church had been planted in the nearby town.

In the autumn of 1997, Georgi was diagnosed with a brain tumor. Even after that, he worked diligently writing his final book, *The Gospel in Bonds* and making plans for the ministry after his passing.

On January 11, 1998, Georgi Petrovich Vins passed from life on earth to his eternal home. Although he had a history of surviving difficulties—including eight years in Soviet prisons and labor camps for his faith, four heart attacks, and heart by-pass surgery in 1990—a brain tumor proved to be his final struggle.

Georgi Vins endured many hardships as he labored for the Lord. But those who knew him well have no doubt that he is finally able to enjoy a time of peace as he worships face to face the Lord he served so well.

> For I am now ready to be offered, and the time of my departure is at hand. I have fought a good fight, I have finished my course, I have kept the faith: henceforth there is laid up for me a crown of righteousness, which the Lord, the righteous judge, shall give me at that day: and not to me only, but unto all them also that love his appearing. (2 Timothy 4:6-8)

APPENDIX 1

DATES AND LOCATIONS OF GEORGI VINS PRISONS & PRISON CAMPS

FIRST PRISON TERM: 3 YEARS 1966-1969

1. Moscow, Lefortovo prison, May 1966-February 1967
2. Prison in Perm, Ural Mountains, March 1967
3. Prison camp "Chepechanka," near Solikamsk, Ural Mountains, March-July 1967
4. Prison camp "Anusha," near Kizel, Ural Mountains, July 1967-May 1969

SECOND PRISON TERM, 5 YEARS 1974-1979

1. Prison in Novosibirsk, Siberia, March 1974
2. Prison in Kiev, Ukraine, April 1974-February 1975
3. Prison camp "Tabaga," near Yakutsk, Siberia, April 1975-February 1979
4. Prison in Tyumen, Siberia, March-April 1979
5. Prison in Moscow, April 1979

Note from Natasha Vins: These are just some major locations of prisons where my father stayed for an extended period of time. When prisoners were transported across the Soviet Union, it usually took many weeks or even months because of huge distances across eleven time zones. While in transit, prisoners were taken by special train cars from one transit prison to a next one in another city where they were kept for several days or weeks. Then another train ride for 12 to 24 hours to a next transit prison. In this way, as my father was taken from Moscow to Urals in 1967 and from Kiev to Yakutsk in 1975, he stayed in dozens of prisons in different cities along the way—it's hard to name them all.

Georgi P. Vins
1928-1998

APPENDIX 2

DOCUMENTS FROM KESTON COLLEGE ON THE PERSECUTION OF THE VINS FAMILY IN THE U.S.S.R.

KESTON NEWS SERVICE

6 JANUARY 1978

Issue No. 47

Information from the CENTRE FOR THE STUDY OF RELIGION AND COMMUNISM
Keston College, Heathfield Road, Keston, Kent,
BR2 6BA. Telephone: Farnborough (Kent) 50116/7

Edited by the Reverend Michael Bourdeaux, M.A., B.D.

LIST OF CONTENTS

SOVIET CRACKDOWN ON CHRISTIAN HUMAN RIGHTS ACTIVISTS*

The Soviet KGB have launched a fresh attack on members of the Helsinki Monitoring Groups in Ukraine and Armenia, according to reports reaching Keston College. The police action coincides ominously with the ending of the present session of the Belgrade Conference reviewing the Helsinki Agreement.

Amongst those affected by the KGB hostilities is Peter Vins, son of Baptist pastor Georgi Vins, who is presently serving a sentence of five years labour camp and five years exile for his religious activities. Peter Vins, an associate member of the Ukrainian Monitoring Group, was arrested on 8 December 1977. He was taken off a Kiev-Moscow train, charged with hooliganism, beaten up and sentenced to fifteen days detention. Bibles found in his possession were confiscated. He has since been sentenced to a further fifteen days detention, allegedly for refusing to work, although prisoners held in prisons (as opposed to those sentenced to labour camps) do not work. In any case, as a result of being beaten up and lack of medical treatment for his injuries, he is said by friends who have visited him to be unfit to work. It appears that on this pretext he could be held indefinitely.

Peter Vins, born 1 May 1956, is probably one of the youngest members of the Monitoring Groups. He has been particularly concerned with the religious situation. He has been informed that a criminal case is being prepared against him. He was warned that he would be prosecuted unless he discontinued his activities with the Helsinki Monitoring Group when he was picked up on the street in Kiev in October. By coincidence or design the KGB investigator on that occasion was the same man who prepared the case against Peter's father.

KESTON NEWS SERVICE

Number 29

Information from the CENTRE FOR THE STUDY OF RELIGION AND COMMUNISM
Keston College, Heathfield Road, Keston, Kent, BR2 6BA.
Telephone: Farnborough (Kent) 50116/7

Edited by the Reverend Michael Bourdeaux M.A., B.D.

LIST OF CONTENTS

2 September 1976

GEORGI VINS

This photograph of Baptist leader Georgi Vins was taken in a labour camp near
Yakutsk, in Siberia, earlier this year. It is believed to be the first
close-up photograph of a prisoner in a Soviet labour camp ever to reach the
West. Vins will reach the half-way point of his five-year sentence on 1 October.
He will then have to serve five years in internal exile before he can return
to his home in Kiev. In June Vins's family were able to pay their annual
visit to him. His mother, Lidia Vins, has said that she wished to take this
opportunity to say farewell to her son, as she herself anticipates that she
could be arrested any day. Now aged 70, she fears she would not survive
another term in labour camp.

Prints of the photograph are available from Keston College.

-4-

VINS APPEAL REJECTED

Further details concerning the case of Georgi Vins, the reform Baptist leader, have been received at Keston College (Centre for the Study of Religion and Communism). The information is taken from a letter of 26 March 1975 which Lidia Vins, Georgi's mother, addressed to the Human Rights Committee and Amnesty International.

→ On 5 March the Vins family delivered a letter to the Supreme Court of the Ukraine in which they drew attention to the illegality of his trial. Vins had himself already appealed to the Supreme Court against his sentence. The court heard his case on 6 March and rejected the appeal. The family were not informed that the hearing had taken place, nor were they told of the decision until 19 March - despite almost daily enquiries. The fact that Vins was in hospital during this times was also 'painstakingly hidden' from them.

The family have also been refused a copy of the official verdict by the Kiev City Court. The judge, a man named Tyshel, claimed that they only wanted a copy in order to send it to the CIA. He described the family as 'enemies of the people' and 'hoodlums'. Now they are being shadowed and the house watched.

→ Lidia Vins appeals for help in opening a re-examination of the case with the participation of a Christian lawyer and representatives from the Supreme Court of the USSR and Amnesty International.

According to an official note of 25 March sent to Lidia Vins, her son is to serve the rest of his sentence in the Yakutsk Autonomous Republic (Eastern Siberia). His health is reported to be 'satisfactory'.

(KNS)

PHOTO CREDITS

Photos on the following pages are from the personal collection of Georgi Vins' daughter, Natasha Velichkin; used with permission: 11, 19-20, 25, 28, 37, 39, 44, 49, 52, 56, 62, 66, 71-72, 76, 80, 84-90, 108, 118, 120-122, 125-130, 134, 146, 154, 156, 158, 164, 182, 192.

Photos on pages 199-205 are from the Georgi Vins Siberian Ministry; used with permission.

Barbed wire border on pages 3, 8, 22, 33, 46, 79, 95, 111, 119, 152 and 189 are from bigstockphotos.com; used with permission.

Brick background on pages 14, 40, 51, 61 are from bigstockphotos.com; used with permission.

Photo on page 12 by Gerald Praschl; used with permission; changed from color photo to black and white photo; licensed under the Creative Commons Attribution-Share Alike 3.0 Unported license (http://commons.wikimedia.org/wiki/File:The_fence_at_the_old_GULag_in_Perm-36.jpg).

Photos on pages 16, 30, 34 102, 103, 167, 186 from bigstockphoto.com; used with permission.

Photos on pages 88 and 89 are from The Keston Archive and Library, Baylor University; used with permission.

Photo on page 92 is from the Library of Congress and is in the public domain. It was obtained from http://www.loc.gov/pictures/item/99615471.

Map on page 104 in public domain.

Photo on page 136 of Viktor Mosha: http://www.ukrweekly.com/archive/pdf2/1982/The_Ukrainian_Weekly_1982-32.pdf.

Photo on page 142 of Fyodor Makhovitsky

Documents on pages 193, 194, and 195 from The Keston Archive and Library. Baylor University; used with permission.

NOTES

Note: See copyright page and photo credits for further citation notes.

CHAPTER 15
1. "Yakutsk—Coldest City on Earth" (English Online; http://www.english-online.at/news-articles/travel/yakutsk-coldest-place-on-earth.htm).

CHAPTER 18
1. Georgi Vins, *Testament From Prison* (Elgin, IL: David C. Cook Publishing, 1975), p. 279; this section written by Lydia Vins in 1975 in a personal report about the trial of her son, Georgi Vins. Used with permission from the Vins family who hold the rights to *Testament From Prison*.

CHAPTER 20
1. Read more about this in Georgi Vins' book *Konshaubi: A True Story of Persecuted Christians in the Soviet Union*. A film titled *Captive Faith* (available through Lighthouse Trails) depicting Georgi Vins' first prison term has also been produced. This film is based on the book *Konshaubi*.

EPILOGUE:
1. Dan Wooding, "Georgi Vins—A Great Warrior For The Gospel" (*Assist News*, http://www.assistnews.net/strategic/s0000014.htm); citing Rick Barry, Former Vice President of Russian Gospel Ministries who was quoting Georgi Vins.

On July 7th, 2004, Georgi Vin's wife, Nadia, went home to be with the Lord.

GEORGI VINS SIBERIAN MINISTRY
ALEXANDER AND NATASHA (VINS) VELICHKIN

I strived to preach the gospel, not where Christ
was named. (Romans 15:20)

Georgi Vins was taken to his heavenly home nearly two decades ago,
but the ministry he committed his whole life to—spreading the
Gospel among the Russian and Ukrainian people—didn't stop with
his passing. Today, his daughter Natasha,* with her husband Alexander, serve as missionaries in Russia bringing the Gospel to remote
and hard-to-reach small villages scattered along two Siberian Rivers.

ALEXANDER & NATASHA (VINS) VELICHKIN

---

*Georgi's younger daughter Lisa also serves on a mission field in Kiev,
Ukraine, along with her husband Scott Carter.

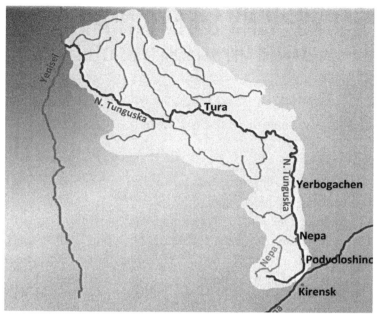

Most of the minority groups along the N. Tunguska and the Nepa Rivers in Siberia have never heard the Gospel. Now is the time to reach them.

Alexander and Natasha's goal is to continue reaching for Christ the small villages along the Siberian Rivers, populated by Russians as well as Tungus and Evenks, native Siberian people groups.

The vast lands of the Siberian north form the remotest and most inaccessible region that covers thousands of square miles. Sparsely populated villages are far removed from the major roads and from each other. In the long months of Siberian winters, the only way to travel is on packed snow roads across land, frozen lakes, and rivers.

During the summer months, locals travel in small boats on the rivers through the beautiful and wild evergreen forests (taiga) or tundra.

The settlements Alexander with his team is trying to reach are small: from 200 to 700 people. They are situated hundreds of miles apart, along the shallow rivers, navigable only for short periods—four to six weeks – in spring after the ice and snow melt.

Siberian Ministry's active outreach takes place right after the rivers thaw until mid June when the water level drops too low to navigate a boat.

Every spring, Alexander and his evangelistic team travel several hundred miles by truck on muddy roads from city Bratsk, where the ministry base is, toward the river where they launch their boats to navigate along the N. Tunguska and the Nepa Rivers.

They stop at every settlement going door-to-door to share the Gospel with villagers, distributing New Testaments and tracts, showing Gospel films, and holding day camps for teenagers and children.

Conditions to get to each village are harsh, as Alexander and his team have to overcome the rough terrain. They have to navigate their boats through the dense Siberian forests as these settlements are separated from each other by hundreds of miles.

Evangelists sleep in tents by the river where overnight temperatures often drop below freezing as the weather changes are unpredictable. Alexander and his team rely on God's protection from attacks by wild animals or unfriendly villagers. Outreach is filled with significant obstacles, but the Lord resolves them one by one in answer to faithful prayers.

Pray for Alexander and his team to speak the mystery of Christ as they ought to speak (Col. 4:2-4). Pray for the Holy Spirit to soften the hearts of these people in the uttermost parts of the earth, in a country where atheism reigned for decades, so that the seed of God's Word might grow. Only our God of miracles can accomplish the impossible to open "the door of faith unto the Gentiles" (Acts 14:27). Please intercede for Alexander and Natasha as they endeavor to fulfill their mission by God's grace.

You may read more about this ministry at www.georgivins.com. On December 21, 2019, Natasha went to be home with the Lord.

CHILDREN OF THE STORM

WRITTEN BY NATASHA VINS—

DAUGHTER OF GEORGI VINS

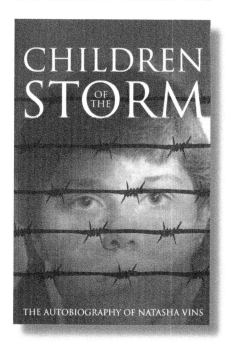

Natasha's father is a leader in the underground church of the Soviet Union. When Georgi Vins is forced to spend time in hiding and in prison, Natasha looks to her beloved grandmother for spiritual guidance, but in her teens Natasha reaches a spiritual crossroads. In a homeland that demands that she embrace communistic ideals and deny the existence of God, will she follow Christ into a life of poverty and hardship, or will she renounce her parents' Christ for the opportunities and open doors which higher education has to offer?

136 Pages | $10.95
Illustrated | Photos
Order through www.lighthousetrails.com

LET THERE BE LIGHT

From evolutionist to creationist

BY ROGER OAKLAND

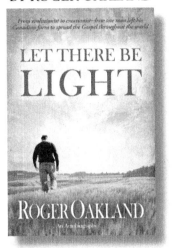

Roger Oakland heads to university with the morals and values of his Christian parents intact. When he enters school, he believes in God as a Creator, but soon exchanges this for Darwinian evolution. After graduation, he begins teaching biology (with an emphasis on evolution) at the same university. Challenged one day by a young Christian student, Roger mocks the whole idea of Creation and God.

Through a series of painful circumstances, including the death of a baby son, he begins searching for answers to life—until one day he has a dramatic experience when hit with the realization that God created everything. Becoming a creationist and later a committed born-again Christian, Roger's life is radically changed. From the wheat fields of Saskatchewan to the classrooms of evolutionary humanism, to a fallen USSR to poverty-stricken villages in Myanmar, Roger shares his message around the world. This apologetics biography will inspire you to give all for the sake of Christ and His Gospel.

224 Pages | $13.95
Illustrated | Photos
Order through www.lighthousetrails.com or any major bookstore outlet.

REMEMBERING

DVDS

CAPTIVE FAITH — BASED ON THE BOOK
KONSHAUBI BY GEORGI VINS
73 MINUTES | $14.95

THE PRINTING
137 MINUTES | $13.95

NIKOLAI
35 MINUTES | $9.95

PRECIOUS & A TRUE REWARD
2 SHORT FILMS
(15 MINUTES EACH) $13.95

COMMUNISM

SOME OTHER TITLES BY
LIGHTHOUSE TRAILS PUBLISHING

BOOKS

Another Jesus (2nd ed.)
by Roger Oakland, $12.95

A Time of Departing
by Ray Yungen, $14.95

Castles in the Sand (a novel)
by Carolyn A. Greene, $13.95

Color, Communism, and Common Sense by Manning Johnson
$12.95

Dangerous Illusions (a novel)
by Carolyn A. Green/Zach Taylor,
$14.95

Faith Undone
by Roger Oakland, $14.95

For Many Shall Come in My Name
by Ray Yungen, $13.95

Foxe's Book of Martyrs
by John Foxe, $14.95, illustrated

How to Protect Your Child From the New Age & Spiritual Deception
Berit Kjos, $14.95

In My Father's House
by Corrie ten Boom, $13.95

Let There Be Light
by Roger Oakland, $13.95

Muddy Waters
by Nanci des Gerlaise, $13.95

Seducers Among Our Children
by Patrick Crough, $14.95

Stolen from My Arms
by Katherine Sapienza, $14.95

Stories from Indian Wigwams and Northern Campfires
Egerton Ryerson Young, $15.95

Strength for Tough Times
by Maria Kneas, $11.95

The Color of Pain
by Gregory Reid, $10.95

Things We Couldn't Say
1st Lighthouse Trails Edition
by Diet Eman, $14.95, photos

The Other Side of the River
by Kevin Reeves, $14.95

Trapped in Hitler's Hell
by Anita Dittman with Jan Markell,
$13.95, illustrated, photos

Up From Slavery
by Booker T. Washington, $12.95

For a complete listing of all our books, DVDs, and CDs, go to www.lighthousetrails.com, or request a copy of our catalog.

Made in the USA
Middletown, DE
20 November 2022

15271223R00119